HISTORIC
CAPE MAY
❖ NEW JERSEY ❖

HISTORIC CAPE MAY

⇝ NEW JERSEY ⇜

THE SUMMER CITY *by* THE SEA

EMIL R. SALVINI

Published by The History Press
Charleston, SC 29403
www.historypress.net

Copyright © 2012 by Emil R. Salvini
All rights reserved

First published 2012

Manufactured in the United States

ISBN 978.1.60949.909.9

Library of Congress CIP data applied for.

Notice: The information in this book is true and complete to the best of our knowledge. It is offered without guarantee on the part of the author or The History Press. The author and The History Press disclaim all liability in connection with the use of this book.

All rights reserved. No part of this book may be reproduced or transmitted in any form whatsoever without prior written permission from the publisher except in the case of brief quotations embodied in critical articles and reviews.

*This book is for Nancy, my muse,
who introduced me to
the Summer City.*

Contents

Preface	9
The Origins of a Resort	11
From 1850 to 1863	29
The Civil War	38
The Lottery of Death	43
The Railroad Comes to Cape May	47
The Cottage Era	50
Railroad Control	56
The Fire of 1869	60
Depression and Reconstruction	64
The Inferno	73
The Road Not Taken	85
Growth After the Fire	93
The *Republic* Era	101
New Jersey Newport	112
Cool Cape May	123
The Great Atlantic Hurricane	137
Peace and Preservation	143
The Winds of Change	149

Contents

"Putting More Christianity in the Patriots"   153
The City Is the Project: Everything Old Is New Again   158
Renaissance   168

Bibliography   177
Index   181
About the Author   189

Preface

As a typical New Jersey native, most of my childhood summers were spent "down the shore." In the 1950s, "the shore" for a North Jersey family meant the area between Sandy Hook and Seaside Heights. Few adventurous souls ventured south of Atlantic City. The resort of Cape May, located forty miles south of Atlantic City at the southernmost tip of the Jersey Cape, was too far "down the shore" to attract North Jersey/New York vacationers.

Once considered the "Queen of the Seaside Resorts," Cape May was a forgotten and unfashionable town known primarily as the home of a large Coast Guard training facility. In the 1950s, Cape May was a collection of aging wooden cottages, boardinghouses and hotels that each summer hosted the remnants of a diminishing but loyal cottage community. The resort's ancient structures survived because no one considered Cape May worth developing. For all but the faithful, the venerable resort, the last stop south on the Garden State Parkway, had slipped into a time warp.

I first explored Cape May twenty years later as a young adult when the rest of the world began discovering the "summer city by the sea." Cape May was experiencing a renaissance that could only be described as miraculous. I immediately fell in love with the old resort and began the research for this book.

Historic Cape May, New Jersey: The Summer City by the Sea is the story of the rise and fall and rise again of the country's first seaside resort—a fantasy city created by whalers, river pilots and speculators and molded by fires and storms. Its two-hundred-year roller coaster ride eventually resulted in Cape May regaining the title of "Queen of the Seaside Resorts."

I wish to thank the following people for their assistance in the completion of this book: my wonderful wife, Nancy, for her patience and hours of companionship while I explored endless museums, libraries and private collections in search of material, as well as for her invaluable input in the design of *The Summer City by the Sea*; and my daughters, Amy and Beth, and my sister, Rosemary, for their constant encouragement. I also acknowledge Jocelyn Thomas Colligan, my editor, who transformed my manuscript into a book; Helenclare Leary, a true fan of Cape May and a longtime resident, whose generosity in sharing her collection and sources with me allowed this effort to be possible; and Ione Williams, recently retired librarian of the Cape May County Historical and Genealogical Society, for her research assistance. My sister Rosemary, Helenclare Leary and Ione Williams have sadly passed away since the first publication of this book. I also wish to thank H. Gerald MacDonald for his photographic expertise and help with many of the images that appear in this book.

For those readers discovering this book for the first time, I hope that you will find it as fresh and informative as when it was first published. I carefully researched the history of this seaside gem and used the original designations for the more than six hundred Victorian era structures in the city, so *The Summer City by the Sea* will never become dated. If a building was built as the George Hildreth Cottage in 1882, that is how I referred to it so that the book would remain accurate as bed-and-breakfast names may come and go. Naturally, change takes place, such as the demolition of the Christian Admiral Hotel (Hotel Cape May) or the addition of the new Convention Hall in 2012, and this edition reflects those changes. Since the original hardcover publication of this book, and after several more works penned by me with an emphasis on the New Jersey Shore, I am proud that the *New York Times* wrote of me, "Mr. Salvini is a historian with solid credentials."

The Origins of a Resort

During most of the eighteenth century, America was a fledgling nation whose citizens lived on farms and in small hamlets and villages. Since there was an abundance of clean water, fresh air and open space, the concept of traveling from one's home for the purpose of relaxing or recreating was for the most part nonexistent. Surviving was the mission of most, and few saw a reason to leave home. The resort industry in America emerged when the country's rapidly developing cities became overcrowded toward the middle of the century. Picture July in an eighteenth-century city; too many horses, flies and people, and not a breeze to be found anywhere. Add ninety-five-degree heat, no air conditioning and an occasional epidemic to the mix, and it's easy to see why anyone who could afford to get away did so.

The city of Philadelphia was the reason Cape May entered the resort business. Established in 1682 as the capital of the Pennsylvania colony, Philadelphia's population had grown to forty-two thousand people by 1790, making it the largest city in the new nation. The city also possessed the busiest seaport and market in North America, and ships traveling down the Delaware River rounded Cape May, New Jersey's southernmost tip, as they headed north for the ports of New York or Boston. It was just a matter of time before some enterprising ship's captain came up with the idea that affluent passengers might pay money to visit the cape during the summer months. Philadelphia had everything but an ocean beach, and Cape May was more than willing to provide one.

Exactly when the first vacationers visited Cape May City is not known, but the antiquity of its resort status is illustrated by the following advertisement that appeared in the *Pennsylvania Gazette* in 1766:

To Be Sold

A Valuable Plantation, containing 254 Acres of Land, Marsh and Swamp, Part of the Swamp cleared, likewise 60 Acres of said Land cleared, the rest well timbered and watered, with a large good two Story House and Kitchen, a very good Barn and Stable and fine Garden; pleasantly situated, open to the Sea, in the Lower Precinct of the County of Cape May, and within One Mile and a Half of the Sea Shore; where a Number resort for Health, and bathing in the Water.

The writer of the ad, Robert Parsons, along with the bay pilots, whale men, farmers and fishermen who occupied the Jersey Cape's coastline, saw the potential of Cape May as a retreat for Philadelphia's emerging merchant class ten years before the American Revolution. After all, the London papers had recently reported that King George III had taken up sea-bathing for his health, and the cape's residents were more than willing to rent out rooms to the fashion-conscious Philadelphians. Benjamin Franklin once said that New Jersey was a cask, tapped on one end by New York and the other by Philadelphia. The "City of Brotherly Love" was about to tap the Jersey seashore, and a new concept was born: the summer vacation.

The village of Cape May was known in the eighteenth and early nineteenth centuries as Cape Island because a small creek separated it from the mainland. There were two means of traveling to the village—by sea and via an arduous land route by stage, wagon or horse.

Until the development of even the crudest of roads to the island, the primary means of transportation was by the bay or sea. A small port existed at Schellinger's Landing at the northeast corner of Cape Island that provided the isolated region with a means to ship lumber and agricultural products and to receive goods from Boston, New York, Philadelphia and more distant ports.

One of the original roads entered the village at Schellinger's Landing, where a ferry conveyed travelers to the island. Another road crossed the peninsula from the village to the bay-side settlements and was known as Cape Island Road.

The first visitors to the village no doubt chose the water route, and it's no mystery why. The hardiest of souls traveled in "jersey or shore wagons," freight wagons that carted sea products from Cape Island to the markets of Philadelphia or Trenton, as well as vacationers on the return trip. "Carted" was the correct term, and this means of travel was for obvious reasons employed by men only. An eighteenth-century poet described colonial roads as follows:

> *Dear George, though every bone is aching,*
> *After the shaking*
> *I've had this week over ruts and ridges,*
> *and bridges*
> *Made of a few uneasy planks,*
> *In open ranks,*
> *Over rivers of mud whose names alone*
> *Would make knock the knees of stoutest man.*

As demand increased, stage routes were established. An advertisement published in the June 30, 1801 edition of the *Philadelphia Daily Aurora* describes one of the earliest:

> *A stage starts from Cooper's Ferry* [now Camden, New Jersey] *on Thursday in every week, and arrives at Cape Island on Friday; it starts from Cape Island on Tuesdays in each week and arrives at Philadelphia the following day.*
>
> *Gentlemen who travel in their own carriages will observe the following directions; Philadelphia to Woodbury is 9 miles, thence to the Glasshouse* [now Glassboro] *10, Malago Mill 10, Lehman's Mill* [near what is today Millville] *12, Port Elizabeth 7, Dennis's Creek* [now Dennisville] *12, Cape May 7, pitch of the Cape 15, is 82 miles and the 18 is open to the seashore. Those who choose water conveyance can find vessels almost any time.*
>
> *Ellis Hughes*

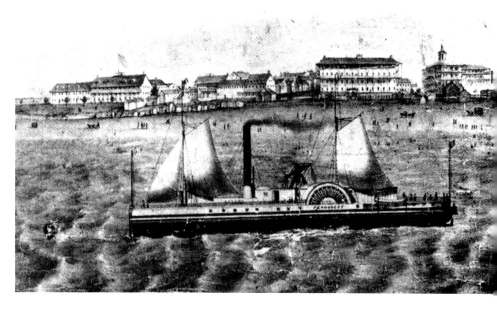

Ocean view of Cape Island from an 1850 map, surveyed and published by P. Nunan. *Left to right*: Old Atlantic, New Atlantic, United States Hotel and Columbia House. Steamships *Penobscot* and *Kennebec* are in the lower half of illustration. *Nunan map.*

The exhausting trip took two days each way, requiring the traveler to board overnight in one of the taverns along the 110-mile trip.

Sailing sloops began regular service between Philadelphia and Cape Island in the first few years of the nineteenth century. Travelers to Cape Island could arrange passage on the *Morning Star*, a sloop that made the trip from Market Street Wharf, Philadelphia, to the resort weekly during the summer season. A schooner, the *General Jackson*, left Philadelphia for Cape Island each Tuesday and left the island for the return trip on Saturdays.

The first visitors to the island were provided with lodging at public houses or taverns. One such establishment was kept by Ellis Hughes, the island's first postmaster and the same enterprising gentleman who placed a stagecoach advertisement in the *Philadelphia Aurora* in 1801. In it, he informed Philadelphians of the following:

SEA SHORE ENTERTAINMENT AT CAPE MAY

The Public are respectfully informed that the Subscriber has prepared himself for entertaining company who use sea-bathing, and he is

The Summer City by the Sea

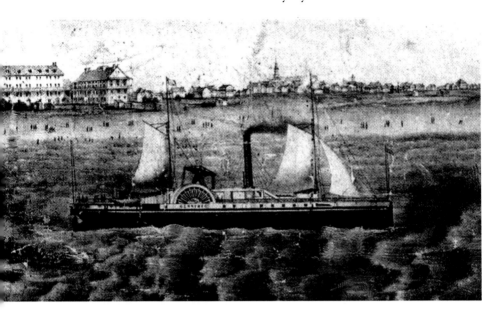

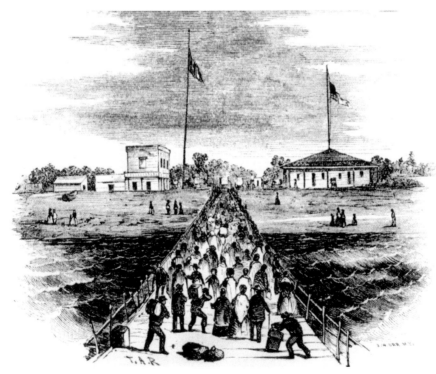

Vacationers disembark from steamer, circa 1859. The steamship landing was located at the terminal of present-day Sunset Boulevard near Cape May Point. Contemporary reports describe hundreds of wagons and carriages awaiting arrival of steamer on a typical summer day. *Cape May County Historical Society.*

> *accommodated with extensive house room, with Fish, Oysters, Crabs, and good Liquors—Care will be taken of gentlemen's Horses.*
>
> *The situation is beautiful, just on the confluence of Delaware Bay with the Ocean, in sight of the Lighthouse, and affords a view of the shipping which enters and leaves the Delaware: Carriages may be driven along the margin of the Ocean for miles, and the wheels will scarcely make any impression upon the sand, the slope of the shore is so regular that persons may wade out a distance. It is the most delightful spot the citizens can retire to in the hot season.*

Taverns and inns were licensed and regulated by the local courts, and Hughes charged the going rate for his services. A night's lodging cost seven cents; breakfast and dinner would set the vacationer back an additional sixty-one and a half cents. Supper could be had for twenty-five cents, and the edge could be taken off the night ocean air with a pint of Madeira wine available at fifty cents. Ellis Hughes's only serious competition at the time was Mills, a lodging house kept by river pilot Ephraim Mills and his wife, Mary. It is estimated that the two establishments could accommodate only thirty lodgers. Many seaside lovers found accommodations at the homes of islanders willing to inconvenience themselves during the "hot season" in order to supplement their incomes. This was no doubt the origin of the love/hate relationship that exists even today in most resort towns between the "townies" and the "summer renters." The extra money was helpful, but giving up your comfortable room to city folk had to have been irritating.

Hughes's tavern evolved into Cape Island's first hotel, Atlantic Hall. *Lippincott's Magazine*, a nineteenth-century publication, described Cape Island and the Atlantic Hall:

> *The customs of those earlier times were very primitive and democratic. Large excursion-parties of gay girls and festive gentlemen would journey together, engaging the right to occupy Atlantic Hall, a desolate barn of a place, fifty feet square, whose proprietor was Mr. Hughes. Then, while the straggling villagers stared, these cargoes of mischief-makers would bear down upon the ocean, ducking and splashing in old suits of clothes brought in their carpet-sacks, and gathering the conditions*

of a fine-appetite. The major-domo of Atlantic Hall, one Mackenzie, would send out to see what neighbor had a sheep to sell; the animal found, all the visitors of the male sex would turn to and help dress it. Meantime, parties of foragers would go out among the farmers ravaging around the neighborhood for Indian corn. When the mutton was cooked and the corn boiled, an appetite would have accumulated sufficient to make these viands seem like the ambrosia of Olympus…At night, when dead-tired after the fiddling and the contra-dances, the barn-like hall was partitioned off into two sleeping-rooms by a drapery of sheets. The maids slept tranquilly on one side of the curtains, the lads on the other. Successive days brought other sports, fishing in the clumsy boats, rides in hay-wagons over the deep white roads, the endless variety being supplied, by the bathing, which was always the same and ever new.

The phrase "desolate barn of a place" refers to the fact that the early hotels were unpainted on the exterior, and the interior walls were void of plaster and lathe.

By 1816, the first wood-burning, side-wheel steamboats joined with the sloops and schooners in the Cape Island/Philadelphia service. The Philadelphia steamboat *Delaware* began regular service in 1816 and traveled from Philadelphia to New Castle, Delaware. Passengers wishing to travel to Cape Island from Baltimore, Washington and points south would board the sloop at New Castle for the resort. This service helped establish Cape May as a favorite resort for the southern states.

As technology improved, steamboats began making the trip from Philadelphia to Cape Island without the assistance of the sloops. The first regular steamboat service was announced in the *Philadelphia Daily Advertiser* in 1819:

*The Steam Boat V*ESTA*, Captain J.H. Burns, will leave the first wharf above Market Street [Philadelphia] at two o'clock, p.m., every Monday and Tuesday during the warm season. She will remain at Cape May but a few hours, and return to Philadelphia. Passengers will be received or landed at Chester, New Castle and Port Penn.*

…To those who are acquainted with Cape May, it is not necessary to say that it is the most economical and comfortable route that can be taken

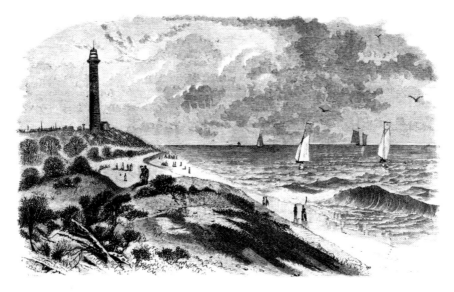

Cape May Lighthouse, circa 1823. The original structure was constructed in 1823. The encroachment of the sea caused the lighthouse to be relocated farther inland in 1847 and again in 1859 to the present site. The lighthouse is open to the public thanks to the restoration project sponsored by the Mid-Atlantic Center for the Arts. *Author's collection.*

> *for pleasure or health, and offering the best surf for bathing. For passage, apply on board, or to JOHN BOWMAN, Jr., No. 3, North Wharves.*

The original steamboat landing was located several miles above the tip of the cape on the bay side. An 1850 map of the resort shows that the landing was later moved closer to Cape May Point, in the vicinity of the terminus of present-day Sunset Boulevard.

A delightful account of a steamboat trip to the island published in *Poulson's Advertiser* in 1823 captures the voyage in wonderful detail. The correspondent wrote his editor from "Cape Town," as he called it, on August 2, 1823:

> *Of the numerous retreats to which ill health, desire of change, or the pursuit of pleasure induces the inhabitants of Philadelphia to resort, none is more famous or more worthy of its fame than the little village from which this letter is dated. I have long considered it as one of the many great causes which the inhabitants of the Middle States have for contentment with their locality that the heats and confinement of a*

The Summer City by the Sea

city life may be so easily exchanged for the salubrity and health of this fashionable watering-place.

There are two routes of reaching it—one by stages which will take you by way of Bridgeton in two days; the other, and by far the preferable and most common conveyance is by one of the steamboats connected with the Baltimore Line, which leaves our city on Monday and Friday mornings, and arrives in the afternoon of the same day.

We started at 5 a.m. in the steamboat *Delaware*, under the command of Captain Whildin...The boat is handsomely fitted up. The deck is long, of good width, perfectly clean and roomy, over which we walked, lounged or sat until 7 o'clock, when we were summoned to a fine breakfast, where plenty of the very best provisions were set before us. Those exquisite, yet rare, luxuries to a traveler, good bread, good coffee, hard Philadelphia butter and well dressed meats, are always to be found on this table to perfection. Every want is supplied by the vigilant waiters and attentive steward, and thus, at a table with, perhaps, seventy or eighty, any one may eat as at home.

After breakfast we passed Fort Mifflin, the Lazaretto, Marcus Hook, the redoubtable fortress on the Pea Patch, Wilmington, and entered the bay. About 12 or 1 we stopped at New Castle for wood and then proceeded without further stoppage. New Castle, which one might suppose a place of some elegance from its situation and importance is as gloomy a looking place as ever I saw...An excellent dinner soon invited our well-prepared appetites to vigorous exertions. The courses displayed the very best cookery, and every sort of drink was ready at call. By the time dinner was discussed, we were almost entirely out of sight of land. Before us nothing was to be seen but boundless water, sky and distant sails of inward and outward bound vessels. Once or twice we enjoyed the beautiful sight of a ship passing us in full sail, bearing off with a strong wind inflating all its canvas.

If the bay happens to be a little rough and the motion of the waves is imparted to the boat, some passengers are affected with seasickness, a trouble in which no one need expect commiseration. Those that are well will only laugh at the indisposed and the others need for themselves all the comfort and warmth they can excite. The cabin, being closer and warmer, is avoided by the indisposed, and the benches and floors of the *deck become couches for the females. All of the preventives and remedies are in circulation, and what just now resembled a gay drawing room looks like a hospital.*

I must not omit to mention that an hour or two after dinner the bell notifies that the captain is ready in the cabin to receive the passage money, six-and-a-half dollars, which covers every expense. At five, six or seven o'clock, according as it has been accelerated or retarded by wind or tide, the boat stops at about 100 yards from the bay side of the Cape, its nearer approach being prevented by the shallowness of the water. A whaleboat is dispatched from the shore which conveys the passengers, and lastly the baggage to wagons collected on the shore, which have understood by a signal from the boat when first in sight how many will be wanted. These convey you over a most delightful road (to my surprise it was only sandy for one-eighth of a mile) three or four miles directly across to Cape Town, or Cape Island, it being insulated by a ditch.

The correspondent mentioned that a lighthouse was being constructed at the extremity of the cape. The finished structure was to be seventy feet high, with five-and-a-half-feet-thick (at the base) walls constructed of brick from Philadelphia.

The lighthouse he mentioned was constructed with funds appropriated by Congress in 1821. It had a revolving light consisting of fifteen lamps, whose flashing mode distinguished it from the fixed and steady light of Cape Henlopen Light, situated across the Delaware Bay. The site of this ancient structure is now underwater, the sea claiming it and forcing the lighthouse to be removed in 1847 to a high bluff, one-third of a mile from the original site. It survived until 1859, when the present Cape May Lighthouse was constructed, standing a short distance from its 1847 ancestor.

Later on in his report, our traveling reporter referred to the medical benefits of the resort:

I have never visited a watering-place where relief was more generally obtained by invalids. Some of my fellow passengers coming down, who were sick, drooping and with no appetite, suffering under various complaints, are now as healthy, brisk and hungry as any here. In short,

The Summer City by the Sea

all are invigorated and at ease. Even hypochondriacs forget their ailments in the general and genial reign of Hygeia.

The nineteenth-century visitors to the seaside were partial to sea-bathing, not to be confused with swimming. Considering the bathing attire of the era, vigorous exercise like swimming was impossible. The ladies were encumbered with woolen or flannel dresses, the accepted bathing garb of the day.

A sea-bather would wade out into the water and jump up and down in joyous abandon; that was it. Medical literature recommended sea-bathing to cleanse the liver and stimulate the circulatory system. While some questioned the healing qualities of the surf, no one could deny that it invigorated the spirit.

Cape Island was now only a day's steamboat ride from one of the country's largest cities, and thousands of sweltering Philadelphians were willing to pay the $6.50 needed to escape the heat.

The Atlantic Hall enjoyed the benefits of being the only hotel on the island for several years, but by the time the traveler wrote that last report (1823), a new hotel had begun to give the Atlantic some real competition.

Thomas H. Hughes, the son of Ellis Hughes, built a three-story boardinghouse in 1816. Another barn-like affair, the frame structure was about one hundred feet long and thirty feet wide. The first floor was used for dining, and the vacationers were boarded in the top two floors. Originally known as the Big House or Large House, the first real competition to the smaller Atlantic Hall could accommodate more than one hundred guests. A vacationer describing the island in 1823 wrote, "The first tavern passed is called the Upper House, kept by M'Kenzie (Atlantic Hall); the next, about the distance of two of our [Philadelphia] squares, is the Large House, by Hughes." The Big House was located at the west end of what is today Washington Street.

Hughes's boardinghouse was officially named Congress Hall during the 1828 summer season. The early nineteenth-century vacationer had not yet been acquainted with what we today would think of as minimum comfort standards, and so Congress Hall, like the Atlantic, was void of paint and plaster. Nobody seemed to mind, for the Large House was filled to capacity each season.

By 1834, Cape Island was being described in the *History and Gazetteer of New Jersey* as follows:

> *A noted and much frequented watering-place, the season of which commences about the first of July and continues until the middle of August or first of September. There are here six boardinghouses, three of which are very large; the sea-bathing is convenient and excellent, the beach offers pleasant drives and there is excellent fishing in adjacent waters. There is a post office.*

The three large hotels referred to were Atlantic Hall, Congress Hall and Cape Island's latest addition, the Mansion House, built in 1832 by Richard Smith Ludlam and located on a tract between Perry and Jackson Streets. Washington Street was opened by Ludlam when he constructed the hotel, and at that time it was one block long and fifty feet wide.

Word of the island's new hotel spread, and before long, it was fully occupied and Cape Island was now beginning to attract fashionable families from New York, Baltimore and Washington, along with the elite of Philadelphia.

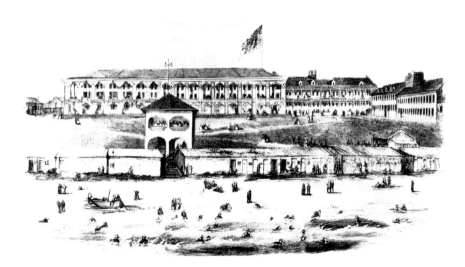

Artist's rendering of Congress Hall and bathhouse in 1858. Originally known as the "Big House," the first structure dated to 1816 and was built by Thomas H. Hughes. A favorite among early nineteenth-century visitors to Cape Island, it was christened Congress Hall in 1828. *Author's collection.*

The Summer City by the Sea

In August 1835, a reporter described the success of the new resort for *Poulson's American Daily Advertiser*:

> *We reached the land's end yesterday, just in time to secure a soft plank in the center of a fine large drawing room with a smart chance of a blanket for bedding. To be plain, the houses are full-crammed, jammed. They have here a Congress Hall, a Mansion House and an Atlantic Hotel, the latter kept by a Saint...There are sundry other smaller establishments for the accommodation of the poor and the blind, but these are the chief houses and they appear to be of the very first order. The Mansion House is the largest and is said to have accommodations for nearly 300 people. Fishing, shooting, (sea) bathing, horsing, constitute the round of recreations and each in its way is enjoyed in higher perfection than almost anywhere else. For a bath in the ocean, no place can compare with it. The houses are all within a step of the great sea, which stretches off before you in all its interminable grandeur.*

In July 1838, Miss Sarah A. McAllister, who was vacationing with her aunt Julie, also made note of the crowded conditions in a letter to her mother from the Mansion House:

> *Hotel crowded; we are obliged to sleep over a half a mile away and come to the hotel for meals; the omnibus came at 7:00 a.m. and did not return until 11:00 p.m.; we had no place to change into our bathing drapes; a lady from the hotel loaned us the use of her room; soon we were given a room in the hotel.*
>
> *Aunt Julie seems to be much benefitted by the bathing. Major Stockton and a lady are at the hotel. Dear Mother, do not worry about my going in too far.*

Sarah went on to mention that most of the guests were horrified about the manner in which a vacationer named Mr. Hales had died, but she assured her mother that it was not by a shark attack.

In spite of the crowded conditions and the growing appeal of the resort, an 1840 census report makes no mention of additional hotels:

> *A favorite watering-place in the southern part of this (Lower) township…It now contains two large hotels (the Atlantic and Congress Hall), three stories high and 150 feet long, and a third one (Mansion House), lately erected, four stories high and 100 feet long, besides numerous other houses for the entertainment of visitors. The whole number of dwellings is about fifty. In summer months the Island is thronged with visitors, principally from Philadelphia, with which there is then a daily steamboat communications. It is estimated that about 3000 strangers annually visit the place.*

These first hotels were plain structures that offered little more than a place to take meals or rest at night. The summer season was short, traditionally July 1 to September 1, and if a hotelkeeper was to show a profit, costs had to be controlled. The happy visitors didn't seem to mind that the hotels were not painted or that the Atlantic Hall and Congress Hall were not even lathed and plastered on the interior walls (a "luxury" introduced by the Mansion House).

The need for additional rooms became more and more apparent, and in 1839, Joseph McMakin, along with his brother, Benjamin, purchased the original Atlantic Hotel in order to expand it. The brothers had experience in operating boardinghouses, both in Philadelphia, where they operated a coffeehouse, and in Cape Island, where they managed the Mansion House for one season.

At the time they purchased the Atlantic, it was described as "a pilot headquarters and in summer a hotel for summer visitors." (As late as 1860, the *Cape May Ocean Wave* noted that the Cape May Pilots held its headquarters at the Old Atlantic Hotel, at the foot of Jackson Street, where all telegraphic news of shipping would be reported.)

It's of interest to note that Joseph McMakin's son, Lewis, stated in 1926 that "tradition said that it [the old Atlantic] had been moved back, as the sea encroached and eroded the gravel bank from some point out among the breakers, but I do not vouch for that story."

The story could be true since it was common in the nineteenth century to move buildings that the ocean threatened to devour. Wood was more expensive than labor, and to this day, many owners of nineteenth-century seaside homes are not entirely sure of their homes' original addresses.

The Summer City by the Sea

Additional evidence supporting the theory is the documented encroachment of the sea. It was recorded by visitors to the resort that the distance from Atlantic Hall to the edge of the beach was 324 feet in 1804. By 1821, the distance was only 174 feet, 8 inches.

Joseph and Benjamin McMakin found the old Atlantic to be a profitable business and immediately purchased a tract of land opposite the original Atlantic. Their new lot fronted the ocean at Jackson Street and extended north as far as Washington Street. They built the New Atlantic on this tract in 1842. Capable of accommodating more than three hundred guests, the New Atlantic was four stories high (the first floor was used as a large dining hall), with a third-story balcony and a massive veranda facing the ocean. A visitor approaching the hotel for the first time would be surprised to see that the McMakins had broken with the local tradition and actually painted the exterior of their building. They chose white, and the hotel proudly displayed its name with eight-foot letters running along the entire front of the building, between the third and fourth floors.

Each new hotel was filled to capacity as soon as it was completed, and by the early 1840s, visitors to Cape Island could choose to stay at one

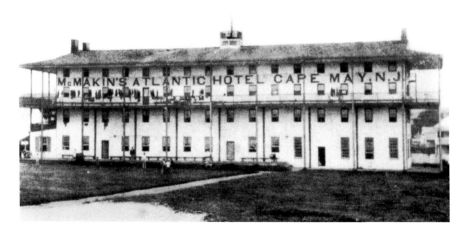

McMakin's Atlantic Hotel stood on the beach between Jackson and Decatur Streets. Eight-foot letters on the outside of the structure located between the third and fourth floors proudly advertised the name of the hotel. Joseph and Benjamin McMakin were the first hotel operators to break with local tradition and paint the exterior of their building (white). *Cape May County Historical Society.*

of the following: Congress Hall, the Old Atlantic, the New Atlantic, the Mansion House, the Centre House (built 1840) and the Ocean House, as well as at a number of small inns and lodging houses. The Mansion House added a music pavilion and ballroom known as the Kersal in the spring of 1847.

The Kersal was quickly put to use when Cape Island received a visit from a nineteenth-century superstar in August of the same year. Henry Clay was considered one of the country's leading statesmen. During his career, he served in the House of Representatives and the Senate and as secretary of state. He was known as the "Great Compromiser," repeatedly assisting in settling disputes over the slavery issue between the North and the South.

His five unsuccessful bids for the presidency did little to tarnish his popularity with the American public. He won their hearts with statements like, "I would rather be right than be President," as well as with his untiring attempts to serve as a peacemaker between the North and South.

As the summer season of 1847 came to a close, the resort was quietly winding down. The hotel orchestras had returned to Philadelphia, and only a few guests remained. Clay chose to visit Cape Island at the end of the season because he was seeking a quiet place to mourn the recent loss of his son in the Mexican-American War. In his own words, "Finding myself in a theatre of sadness, I thought I would fly to the mountain top and descend to the waves of the ocean, and by meeting with the sympathy of friends, obtain relief to the sadness which encompassed me."

This was not to be, for news of his upcoming visit caused a frenzy the likes of which the resort had never seen. As the news spread, the hotels began to fill up as if July 1 had just arrived. Crowds traveled from the southern and middle states, and an envoy of dignitaries, including Horace Greeley, hired a special steamboat to take them from New York to Cape Island. The New Yorkers' mission was to entice Clay to visit their metropolis. Not to be outdone, envoys were sent from Trenton, Philadelphia and New Haven.

Clay decided to stay at the Mansion House, much to the joy of the proprietor, Richard Smith Ludlam. Arrangements were made by the hotel to have a band travel with Clay on the steamboat that delivered him

The Summer City by the Sea

from Philadelphia. He gave a speech in the new Kersal, and a witness reported that he held the crowd spellbound. Clay took a sea-bath twice a day, during which he was hounded by frantic female fans hoping to shear one of his locks as a souvenir (hair wreaths were popular during this era). Clay stayed at the resort for almost two weeks, and it was said that his hair was quite short when he returned to Washington.

The statesman thanked the many envoys who made the journey to Cape Island but graciously declined their invitations, stating that he needed the time to mourn his son. His choice of Cape Island reinforced the resort's position as the major seaside retreat in the country. (While it is well documented that Clay stayed at the Mansion House, the local legend that believes that the "A. Lincoln" who visited the old hotel on July 31, 1849, was Abraham Lincoln has been debunked. The hotel register

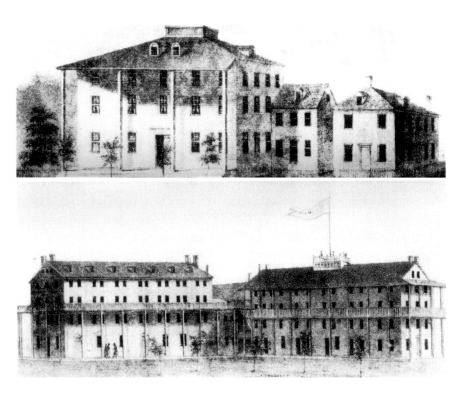

White Hall (above) and the Columbia House (below), both renderings from the 1850 Nunan map. Built in 1846, the Columbia House fronted on the west side of Ocean Street and survived until 1878. White Hall was the ancestor of the Hotel Dale, an early twentieth century African American Hotel. *Nunan map*.

shows an A. Lincoln and wife from Philadelphia in room 24, but Lincoln scholars claim that the future president was a thousand miles west of Cape May on that day, filing an affidavit for a client in Illinois. Add to that the recent discovery that a grocer named Abel Lincoln resided in Philadelphia during the time the register was signed, and many wonder if the supporters of the myth have confused the Great Emancipator with the green grocer.)

The success of the resort continued to be fueled by the improvements made in transportation. Steamboat transportation to the island became more organized, and vacationers found it easier and more comfortable to travel to Cape Island. As more steamboat operators competed for the trade, the price of a trip went down. Larger steamboats traveling between New York City and Philadelphia made regular stops at Cape Island, and by 1850, these lines had reduced the cost of the Philadelphia/Cape Island voyage to one dollar. The trip from New York to Cape Island was now just over twelve hours. Steamboats with names like *Traveler*, *Napoleon*, *America* and *Mountaineer* traveled up and down the Delaware during the summer season, filling the hotels to capacity. The steamboat landing was improved, and a saloon soon greeted the passengers as they disembarked.

By the 1850 season, the hotel list had grown with the addition of the American House, Delaware House, Franklin House, Columbia Hotel, Commercial House, Madison House, New Jersey House, White Hall, Cape Island House and Hughes Hall. (White Hall survived into the twentieth century and was eventually converted in 1911 to the Hotel Dale, an African American hotel. Notables such as Booker T. Washington and W.E.B. Du Bois were guests of the hotel.)

From 1850 to 1863

By the 1850 summer season, Cape Island had grown prosperous and was the nation's most famous seaside resort. It held dominion over competing resorts for half a century due mainly to its location, which permitted easy access by ocean and bay transportation. In addition, the tiny resort was blessed with a broad, smooth sandy beach that gently sloped into the sea and was tailor-made for sea-bathing. The ocean and bay provided the village with a constant cooling breeze that was highly prized in an era that lacked air conditioning.

Confidence had reached an all-time high when in February 1852 a group of Philadelphia and southern New Jersey investors joined together with John West to incorporate the Mount Vernon Hotel Company. Construction on the hotel began the same year. Situated on a ten-acre plot in the sparsely developed west end of town (the property began at what is today Broadway and extended five hundred feet west along the oceanfront), the hotel was to be the largest seaside hotel in the world.

By September 1853, the Mount Vernon was about one-third complete, and it became the subject of an article in the *Illustrated London News*. Although portions of the story resemble a public relations release, its contemporary view of the hotel warrants a look:

Historic Cape May, New Jersey

The Mount Vernon, Cape May, N.J. (US)

This magnificent establishment is not situated in a large city nor in any populous neighborhood, but at the quiet watering-place of Cape May in New Jersey…

The style is palatial; the dimensions far exceed those of any hotel in England. The building consists of a front, four stories in height and 300 feet long, and two wings extending backwards at right angles, of similar height, but each 506 feet in length.

Enclosed between the wings is a large garden, planted with beautiful shrubs, and having in the middle a fountain of elegant design and elaborate construction. This garden is open at its southern extremity to the sea, between which and the hotel itself a smooth and sloping sandy beach intervenes.

…Balconies and verandahs are continued round the structure in front of each story; and some idea of the great extent of the whole pile may be formed from a statement of fact that there is one mile and a half of verandah…

The hotel is intended to accommodate 3500 guests [it accommodated about 2,100 at this unfinished stage]. *The visitor is charged two dollars and a half per day. This included his lodging and his meals; but not his wine, his washing, and his servants… They are not expected to receive gratuities; but the guest who wishes to be waited on well does not omit to win the good graces of the waiter by a conciliatory fee…The best things will be passed on to someone more liberal, and the ungenerous is likely to be dinnerless…*

The establishment is lighted with gas…and so extensive is the building that it contains 125 miles of gas and water pipes, indeed, it has pipes enough in it to supply a moderately sized town.

The Mount Vernon possessed an immense dining hall that was 425 feet long and 60 feet wide. More than forty gas-burning chandeliers illuminated the spacious hall in which a guest reported counting more than 750 people dining on one occasion. The hotel contained a barbershop, a stable and a carriage house. Guests seeking a day of rest from the rigors of sea-bathing could enjoy the tenpin alleys and pistol galleries. There

The Summer City by the Sea

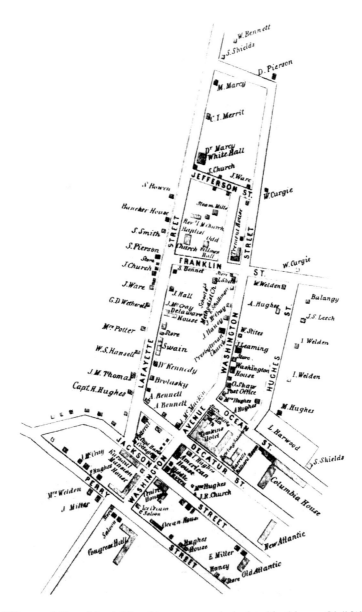

An 1850 map of Cape Island. The old town center is depicted in this pre–Civil War street map. The principal streets that ran from the ocean to Washington Avenue were Perry, Jackson, Decatur and Ocean. Major hotels identified are Congress Hall, Old Atlantic, New Atlantic, Columbia House and the Mansion House. *Nunan map.*

was an archery tent, quoit pitching area and a Hippodrome ring for the ladies. A horse railroad carried guests between the hotel and the beach.

By the beginning of the 1856 season, the hotel was still under construction. New owners Philip Cain and Frank T. Foster purchased the establishment from the original proprietor, Samuel Woolman, and they predicted that the Mount Vernon would be completed by the opening of the 1857 season. They advertised their partially completed hotel as "[t]he magnificent hotel, the largest and most comfortable one in the world…It being capable of accommodating 2100 people comfortably and dining 3000…board $2 per day."

Business was brisk, and many guests planned on returning to the hotel when it was completed next season. This was not to be. On September 5, 1856, the Mount Vernon fell victim to the plague of nineteenth century America: fire.

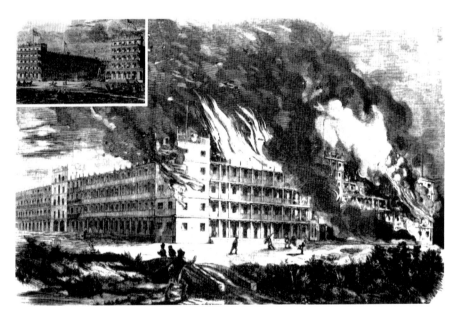

The Mount Vernon Hotel fire. Promoted as the world's largest hotel, with accommodations for more than 2,100 guests, the partially completed structure burned to the ground on September 5, 1856. The Mount Vernon fire was the first of many that would plague Cape Island during the nineteenth century. The mammoth hotel contained more than 125 miles of gas and water pipes. *Inset*: The Mount Vernon as it would have appeared upon completion. The dining hall of this gigantic structure was said to have had more than forty gas-burning chandeliers. *From* Frank Leslie's Illustrated Newspaper, *September 20, 1856.*

The Summer City by the Sea

The front of the massive building was the first to ignite (cause unknown), and the flames quickly spread through the dining hall and guest rooms. Within an hour and a half, the Mount Vernon was just a memory. Since the official summer season had ended four days earlier, the loss of life was mercifully low. Lost in the blaze, though, was co-owner Philip Cain, with four of his children and a housekeeper.

The Mount Vernon fire reduced the number of rooms available to Cape Island visitors by 2,100. Many historians believe that the fire marked the end of the resort's charmed existence. As the second half of the nineteenth century unfolded, Cape Island was unchallenged as the grand lady of seaside resorts. However, a series of events would soon threaten its supremacy as the country's most stylish retreat.

Steamships continued to arrive daily during the summer season, and hotels were overflowing. The resort's control of the Delaware River/Bay transportation monopoly guaranteed it a steady stream of summer visitors from the Quaker City. In the era of stagecoaches and poor roads, Cape Island was the most successful resort because it was the most convenient.

By 1851, six private roads had been surveyed and opened as public streets: Decatur, Ocean, Washington, Hughes, Franklin and Jefferson. These streets, along with the original town thoroughfares of Perry, Jackson and Lafayette Streets and Washington Avenue, linked the

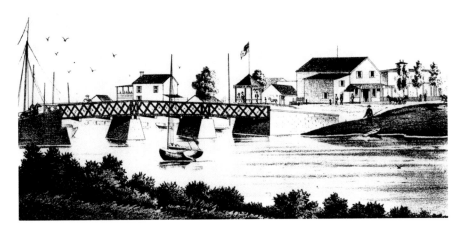

Schellinger's Landing, 1878. Pictured on the right is Joseph Schellinger's coal and general store. The bridge (left) replaced the ferry at the landing in the early 1850s and created a new land route to the island. *From* Woolman & Rose Atlas, *1878.*

neighborhoods of the bustling village. The year 1851 was when the borough was incorporated as Cape Island City.

In 1852, the Cape Island Turnpike Company laid out a straight road that connected the steamboat terminus to Cape May. Known today as Sunset Boulevard, the turnpike replaced the older, primitive road that led from the bay to the resort. (The turnpike charged a toll into the twentieth century.) Another improvement was a permanent bridge that replaced the ferry at Schellinger's Landing and opened up the land route to the resort.

Congress Hall was remodeled in 1854. A guest of the hotel wrote, "What else can it be but grand? At night, when this hall is cleared of its tables and chairs, and hundreds of gas jets are brilliantly burning and flickering and the gay and the elite are flushed with the giddy dance, then you behold a hall-scene, beautiful and fair." The new hotel was 250 feet long and 42 feet wide, with a wing that measured 90 feet by 42 feet. The same year marked the completion of the telegraph line connecting the resort with Camden City and Philadelphia. Cape Island City was now linked to the world. The resort was alive with not only guests but also the carpenters, hack drivers, tinsmiths, painters, storekeepers and tailors a thriving watering place required.

The summer season of 1855 brought the first visit from a sitting United States president, Franklin Pierce. The city officials gave a grand reception for Pierce, and thousands of visitors crowded the streets in the hopes of getting a glimpse of their president. His visit attests to the status of the resort and was no doubt reported in the city's first newspaper, the *Cape May Ocean Wave*, which published its first issue in 1854. The paper, under the guidance of editor and publisher Joseph Leach, carried Philadelphia and New York news fresh off the new telegraph wire. In addition, a local reporter gathered and reported city and county news.

Along with the local gossip, the *Cape May Ocean Wave* announced more ominous national news: the growing tension between the slavery and antislavery factions was accelerating at a disturbing rate. One year before his visit to the island, President Pierce had supported and signed into law the Kansas-Nebraska Act. This new law, which allowed settlers in the country's new territories to decide for themselves whether to permit slavery, posed a threat to the uneasy slavery truce established by compromises in 1820 and 1850 and brought the country one step closer to war.

The increasing tension between the North and South could only prove disastrous for a seaside resort located south of the east–west boundary of the Mason-Dixon line. Cape Island depended on both regions of the country for its survival. The steamboats that had operated for years on the Philadelphia/Cape Island line continued to stop at New Castle, Delaware, which provided the link between Cape Island and the South. The prominent cities of Richmond, Savannah, Baltimore and Washington, possessing no shore resorts that equaled Cape May, had adopted the Summer City as their own.

As the momentum toward war accelerated and each day's news on the wire caused more alarm, several unrelated events occurred that further threatened the stability of the resort.

In March 1852, the same year the Mount Vernon Hotel Company was organized, a seemingly insignificant development took place that would ultimately change the way the world vacationed. The New Jersey legislature issued a charter for a railroad to be built from Camden City to Absecon Island, some forty-five miles up the coastline from Cape Island and only sixty miles from Philadelphia.

A railroad linking Philadelphia with the Jersey shore had been a dream of Dr. Jonathan Pitney since 1830. Pitney had known for years that Cape Island's success was due in part to the transportation monopoly it controlled and that the established resort was too far south to compete with a new, more conveniently located resort. The resourceful physician organized a group of prominent South Jersey businessmen and convinced them that a seaside resort, linked by rail to Philadelphia, would be an unrivaled success. The Camden and Atlantic Railroad was organized and promptly constructed. On July 1, 1854, a train full of investors, newspapermen and Philadelphia bigwigs arrived in Pitney's dream village, Atlantic City.

Later in the century, writers would praise the visionaries who recognized the many natural benefits that Atlantic City possessed and how they had the foresight to make these wonders available to the world. The truth of the matter was that Absecon Island (Atlantic City) lies in as straight a line possible from the Quaker City to the Atlantic Ocean, and that's why the site was selected.

Pitney and the organizers of the railroad bought land for pennies that would skyrocket in value when their railroad was completed. More than one thousand acres of prime beach land, and property along the path of the new railroad, previously purchased by the railroad's land company for $10 per acre, would soon sell for $300 per acre. The consortium could take its profits from the sale of the land, and new landowners would guarantee profits for the railroad. It was a win-win situation.

Now, it should not be said that the town fathers of Cape Island did not recognize the potential threat from the upstart resort. By 1850, there were about nine thousand miles of railroad track in the United States. This would increase to thirty thousand miles by the end of the decade. Cape Island and the rest of Cape May County knew that a railroad link to Philadelphia and the northern section of the state was imperative. Pitney and his crew were about to tap into the older resort's goldmine. Atlantic City had already begun work on the United States Hotel, which was to become the country's finest resort hotel. Atlantic City's marketing plan would be simple: why take a steamboat ride to Cape Island that took a full day when the new railroad was so fast you could visit Atlantic City and return to Philadelphia the same day?

Although the railroad charter from Camden to Atlantic City was obtained in only two years, the efforts of Cape May supporters to extend the railroad to the Cape May peninsula proved as long and arduous as the unpaved roads leading to the aging resort.

The promoters of the new charter found themselves entangled in a quagmire of politics and special interests. The New Jersey legislature had, in 1832, granted an exclusive right-of-way through the state to the Delaware and Raritan Canal and the Camden and Amboy Railroad. Under the provisions of the 1832 grant, no railroad line could be chartered in the state without the consent of these companies.

In the meantime, fire had taken its toll on Cape Island. The Mount Vernon Hotel fire had reduced the number of available rooms by 2,100. One year later, in 1857, the Mansion House, including its new music hall, burned to the ground. This further reduced the room space by another 300.

Despite the obstacles of transportation and fire, there were bright spots during the decade, and the resort experienced some growth. In

The Summer City by the Sea

1858, President James Buchanan paid a visit to the island. The same year witnessed the construction of another hotel, Tontine Hall, located on the northwest corner of Lafayette and Jackson Streets.

The resort was still attracting visitors from the south, though that was soon to change. One observer counted more than three hundred horse-drawn conveyances of different types at the steamboat landing at one time, all in wait to transfer arriving guests to their hotels. The wealthiest guests to the island would bring their own stately carriages, along with magnificent teams of horses, complete with gold and silver harnesses.

The hotels were the centers of resort activity. They competed with one another to provide the best in entertainment and recreational activities. Dances, or hops, were popular events, and the best bands from Philadelphia and New York were brought in to serenade guests. The highlights of the season were the Gala Balls that took place in immense hotel dining rooms. The elite of the North and South would dance the night away in the magical light of a hundred flickering gas chandeliers.

After the dance, they would sit on the moonlit veranda and ponder the approaching storm that would soon change their lives forever.

The Civil War

In October 1859, John Brown and twenty-one of his followers seized the federal arsenal at Harper's Ferry, Virginia, with the intent of establishing an abolitionist republic in the Appalachians. Brown believed that the slaves in the vicinity would join his small band of men and was prepared to arm them with hundreds of rifles and pistols that he had carted to Harper's Ferry. His plan of organizing fugitive slaves and abolitionist whites ended when the slaves refused to rebel and the angry townspeople stormed the arsenal and captured Brown. The abolitionist agitator that author Herman Melville referred to as "the meteor of the war" was sentenced to death by hanging. As he was escorted to the gallows, Brown handed a note to a guard that predicted that "the crimes of this guilty land will never be purged away but with blood."

The incident deeply divided the nation. Southerners felt that Brown was a murderer and traitor. The *Richmond Whig* echoed the popular opinion of the South when it noted, "The miserable old traitor [Brown] belongs to the gallows." The majority of Southerners believed that the North's sanction of Brown's actions proved there was no place for the South in the Union. Northerners believed that he was nothing short of a saint. Longfellow, in writing of Brown's execution, noted prophetically that "this is sowing the wind to reap the whirlwind, which will soon come."

On November 6, 1860, Abraham Lincoln was elected president. On December 13 (seven days before South Carolina seceded from the union),

The Summer City by the Sea

Joseph Leach, publisher and editor of the *Cape May Ocean Wave*, reported to his readers, "Dissolution of the Union…Suffice it to say, that the peril is imminent…we greatly fear the worst, while we still faintly hope for peace…The secession feeling in the South is deepening and widening, and there is no use in attempting to disguise the fearful aspect of the present dreary and beclouded political skies."

At a Grand Union meeting held on December 27 at Cape Island's city hall, town officials and citizens pledged their support to the union. The city that played host to thousands of wealthy Southern planters and merchants each year had been forced to take sides.

The Civil War began in the early morning hours of April 2, 1860, when the forces of the Confederacy opened fire on the Federal garrison at Fort Sumter in the Charleston, South Carolina harbor. No one involved could have realized that this was the beginning of four years of bloody warfare.

Fear spread throughout the country. Joseph Leach issued a warning to Cape May county farmers that the coming summer season would no

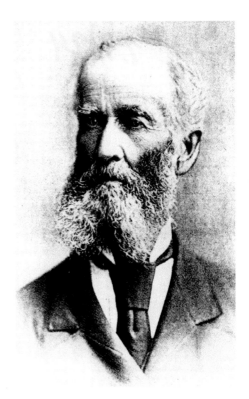

Joseph S. Leach, publisher and editor of the *Cape May Ocean Wave* and a staunch supporter of the Union. He was born in Shutesbury, Massachusetts, on March 30, 1816, and died at his residence in Cape May City on August 9, 1892. *From* History of Cape May County, *1897.*

doubt be a lean one for the resort. He cautioned that the war would cause financial crisis and drive the wealthy Southern patrons away from the famous watering place. He advised them to "plant accordingly."

The war escalated, and Cape Island fell on hard times. Its Southern patrons disappeared overnight, in most cases never to return. (It is estimated that Southerners spent more than $50,000.00 at the resort in the year before the war. To put that in perspective, a laborer made $0.90 per day in 1860, and a four-room apartment could be rented for $4.45 per month.)

By 1861, hotel proprietors were running advertisements that offered reduced rates due to "the pressure of the times." The Cape Island Home Guard was formed, and the old cannon "Long Tom" was refurbished to defend the island from attack. The *Cape May Ocean Wave* continued to report the war news and cautioned its readers that "the southern fire-eaters inform us, they intend to capture Washington."

The city council feared that some of the fire-eaters might attempt to torch the Northern resort. Mysterious fires erupted throughout the village, including one on October 27, 1862, at the United States Hotel. Though it was discovered and extinguished, panic spread throughout the highly flammable wooden city. The council appropriated $1.25 per night to pay two city watchmen to be on duty from 8:00 p.m. to 6:00 a.m. A $500.00 reward was offered for the arrest of the person or persons who set fire to the United States Hotel.

As the anxiety increased, a Vigilance Committee was formed by "some of the best citizens of the island," and this group began a secret watch that replaced the public watchmen.

The telegraph that connected the resort to Philadelphia and the outside world had been abandoned on the eve of the war, and Cape Island became isolated from the North and feared a Southern invasion. (The line was eventually restored when Waters B. Miller, a member of the Cape Island Board of Freeholders, convinced New Jersey's Governor Olden that the telegraph would be an invaluable tool in maintaining communications with Federal vessels off the Capes of Delaware and New Jersey.)

As the war lingered on, the *Cape May Ocean Wave* reported numerous incidents that illustrated the resort's precarious position—a pro-Union

The Summer City by the Sea

New Jersey village situated far enough south to be on the same latitude as Washington and below Baltimore:

> CAPE ISLAND, N.J. JULY 25, 1861:
>
> *The firing of cannon was heard from the direction of Cape Henlopen. It was night so the flashes of the cannon could be seen. A large crowd gathered on the beach and lawn of Congress Hall. Some feared an invasion or bombardment. The knees trembled, the hearts throbbed and the countenances grew pale of many timid persons who feared it was a privateer nearing our shores for the purpose of bombarding Cape Island.*

The fearful islanders went to sleep convinced that a Southern invasion was imminent. The mystery was solved the next evening when a boat arrived from the breakwater and informed the islanders that an inaccurate dispatch had been received at Lewistown (Lewes), Delaware, proclaiming the Federals victors of the Battle of Bull Run near Manassas, Virginia. The patriots at Lewistown had given a grand cannon salute in honor of the Union. The article concluded: "How indignant those fellows must have felt on learning that it was an idle rumor." (The first Battle of Bull Run took place on July 21, 1861, and was a major victory for the Confederacy.)

Although the island's hotel owners dearly missed the Southern clientele that once filled their now empty establishments, Joseph Leach and his *Ocean Wave* saw to it that their commercial requirements came second to their support of the Union. Articles such as the following were common:

> CAPE ISLAND, N.J. 1862:
>
> *"Sir," a friend writes from Cape May, "for some days past, the flag over Congress Hall has not been flying. Upon inquiry, we learn that the proprietors had been waited on by some of the secession sojourners at the house hailing from Baltimore, and informed that they would not stay in the house, if the stars and stripes were kept waving over it. In deference to their sensibilities, the flag was struck. Can this possibility be true?...Loyalty."*

The owners of Congress Hall responded immediately and "unhesitatingly denounced the article" as a "base, willful and malicious lie, and put in circulation for no other purpose than to injure our business."

Hotels continued to fall into disrepair, with little funds available for carpenters and painters. Investors refused to risk money in a village that depended so heavily on the South. The *New York Herald* published an article describing the once stately resort as "the collection of hotels and cottages known by the dignified title of 'the City of Cape Island'" and noted that "the same glorious old ocean still breaks upon the strand and the same paint-less, graceless, and comfortless hotels still occupy the same shade-less localities." To make matters worse, the resort's transportation monopoly was crippled as the government began to claim the steamboats and schooners to use as troop transports.

Still, the island attempted to maintain the illusion of business as usual. In the year 1862, the nation reeled under the news of the Battles of Shiloh, Antietam and Fredericksburg. The August 14, 1862 *Ocean Wave* carried this statement: "Men of Cape May, in a few days I expect to drop my pen and take up the sword, and go forth to battle for my Country. Come and go with me! Duty calls you! Our Union must be saved and traitors conquered. Let those who will volunteer send me their names. I hope to have twenty or thirty go with me…J. Granville Leach, Reporter, Ocean Wave." (Josiah Granville Leach was the eldest son of the *Cape May Ocean Wave* publisher Joseph S. Leach. He "took up the sword," eventually achieved the rank of second lieutenant and was cited for bravery in the Battle of Fredericksburg, Virginia.)

That same year, the *Cape May Ocean Wave* ran a story noting that "the grandest hop that has yet taken place on the Island this summer, came off at Congress Hall." The editor then somberly and candidly reported that "the dances show a scarcity of young men. Thousands, who other seasons 'tipped the light fantastic toe' in our ball-rooms, are sleeping in heroes' graves, or now march, instead of dance, to the music of fife and drum, upon the soil of rebeldom."

Regardless of the outcome of the war, few believed that the resort of Cape Island could weather the storm.

The Lottery of Death

No discussion of Cape May and the Civil War would be complete without a mention of Henry W. Sawyer and the wartime incident that, for a brief moment, made him a national hero. A carpenter by trade, Henry Sawyer moved to Cape Island in 1848.

When the Civil War erupted, he was one of the first locals to volunteer for service. He traveled to Trenton to meet with the governor and offer his services. The New Jersey forces had not yet been organized, so Sawyer was assigned to a Pennsylvania unit. He quickly distinguished himself and rose from private to second lieutenant in only sixty days. He returned to Cape May at the conclusion of his three-month enlistment but stayed only a short while.

Eager to serve his country and unknowingly approaching his date with history, Sawyer contacted the governor and once again offered his services. On February 19, 1862, he was assigned to the First New Jersey Cavalry, Company D, as a second lieutenant. By October of the same year, he had advanced to the rank of captain of Company R.

On June 9, 1863, the largest cavalry battle of the Civil War took place at Brandy Station, Virginia. Jeb Stuart's famed horsemen engaged the Union cavalry in a bloody battle in which twenty-one thousand men fought along the Rappahannock River for more than twelve hours. Although the Confederates narrowly held the day, the Union cavalry came away with a bolstered ego. They had taken on the infamous Rebel cavalry and fought them to a standoff.

Among the wounded was a Union cavalry officer named Henry Sawyer. He was captured by the Confederates and sent to Libby Prison in Richmond, Virginia. The events that followed—which would make wonderful fiction were they not true—made Sawyer the topic of conversation from Richmond to Washington.

On July 6, the Rebel prison officials gathered all Union captains imprisoned at Libby. Sawyer and his fellow officers believed that the officials were assembling them to discuss a general pardon and release. The Northern officers' anticipation turned to dread when they were told the grim purpose of the meeting. They were informed that the Rebel war department had decided to execute two captains in retaliation for the executions of two Confederate officers captured in the North by Union general Ambrose Burnside.

The victims were to be chosen by lot, a "Lottery of Death" as it became known. All of the officers' names were written on small squares of paper and put in a box. The first two men chosen were to be shot. After being given a choice, the officers requested that Reverend Mr. Brown of the Sixth Maryland perform the somber task of picking the names.

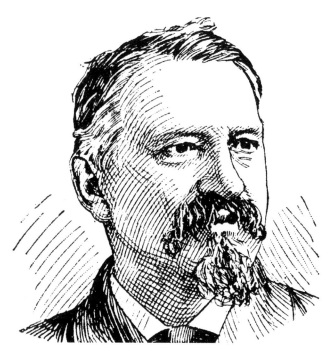

Henry W. Sawyer was a Civil War hero and early Cape May pioneer. For a brief period of time, Sawyer became an unwilling player in a drama that captivated the nation. *From History of Cape May County, 1897.*

The Summer City by the Sea

The first name chosen was Captain Henry W. Sawyer of the First New Jersey Cavalry, and the second was Captain Flynn of the Fifty-first Indiana. The *Richmond Dispatch* reported, "Sawyer heard it with no apparent emotion, remarking that someone had to be drawn, and he could stand it as well as anyone else. Flynn was very white and depressed." Sawyer and Flynn were separated from their comrades and told that the execution would take place in eight days on July 14.

Sawyer realized that his only chance to live lay in political intervention. His captors allowed him to write to his wife at Cape Island, provided they inspect the letters. He wrote her of his dire situation and that the Confederates would allow her and their children to visit him before the execution. "My situation is hard to be borne, and I cannot think of dying without seeing you and the children…I am resigned to whatever is in store for me, with the consolation that I die without having committed any crime." He implored her, "If I must die, a sacrifice to my country, with God's will I must submit; only let me see you once more and I will die becoming a man and an officer, but for God's sake, do not disappoint me."

She did not fail him and quickly brought the matter to the attention of influential friends in Cape Island. They traveled to Washington and petitioned President Lincoln to intercede. He did, instructing Secretary of War Edwin Stanton to place in close confinement two Rebel officers not below the rank of captain.

Stanton had two special prisoners in mind. The first was General John H. Winder, son of Confederate provost-marshal General William H. Winder, and the second was General William Henry Fitzhugh Lee, son of General Robert E. Lee himself. As fate would have it, Lee's son was captured at the Battle of Brandy Station the same day Sawyer was taken prisoner.

Word was sent to the Confederacy: execute Sawyer, Flynn or any other innocent captive, and Lee and Winder would be shot in retaliation. The story was reported in the national newspapers, and the "Lottery of Death" captured the country's interest. The Southern population was outraged at the Northern threat, but many realized that the Confederate's lottery was equally unjust.

Needless to say, the executions did not take place, and in March 1864, Captain Sawyer was exchanged for Lee's son. Unfortunately for Captain

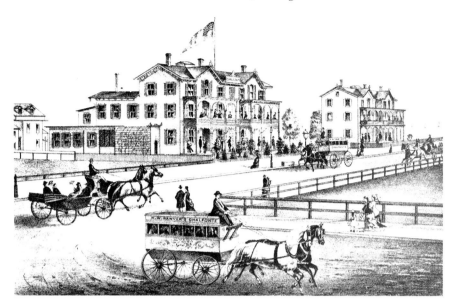

Henry Sawyer's Chalfonte Hotel was built in 1875. Located on Howard and Sewell Streets, the hotel is still in operation today. The wagons pictured in this illustration, drawn two years after the hotel opened, transported guests between the city and the steamboat landing. *From Woolman & Rose Atlas, 1878.*

Flynn, the long captivity had caused a deterioration of his health and spirit, and he died six months after his release from Libby Prison.

Sawyer returned to Cape Island and his wife via a hero's welcome in Trenton. He returned to his beloved First New Jersey and eventually achieved the rank of colonel, serving the regiment until it was disbanded in 1865. The Colonel, as he became known, built the Chalfonte Hotel in Cape May in 1875 and operated it for seventeen years. The hotel still stands on Howard and Sewell Streets.

It was said that there existed no man, woman or child in Cape May who did not know by heart the tale of the "Lottery of Death."

The Railroad Comes to Cape May

By the summer of 1863, the nation had suffered through three years of bloody carnage with no end in sight. As news of the Confederate defeat at Gettysburg reached the residents of Cape Island, an event took place that would change the resort forever. The hopes of the once bustling watering place came alive as the final railroad tracks of the Cape May and Millville Railroad, connecting the island with Philadelphia and the rest of the world, were completed. (The New Jersey legislature had granted the Millville and Glassboro Railroad Company the right to complete the missing link from Millville to Cape Island by a special act approved on March 9, 1863.)

Local resident Amelia Hand wrote in her diary, "We at last have a railroad from Cape Island to Philadelphia, and August 26th the cars made a trip for the first time…the route was performed in three and a half hours, quite an improvement over our old way of going to Philadelphia which took the most part of one day." She went on to note that two trains a day "bring us as near to a large city as one need wish be."

Several months before the arrival of the railroad, the ever-vigilant Joseph Leach warned the city that the long-awaited railroad and its promise of prosperity required a commitment from the island's citizens. He cautioned that the railroad was only a means of transporting vacationers to the resort. The city must provide "proper inducements to attract them, and render their stay pleasant." He candidly reminded the town that "it has been often said, by our own citizens who have visited other watering-places, that in the way of improvements, we are fifty years behind the times…and if there was ever a time when we need to be awake on this point, it is now."

He went on to compare Cape Island with the new resort of Atlantic City, which already offered wide streets and sidewalks. With such modern improvements available, why would anyone "be satisfied with being compelled to walk single file, through mud and water, and pay for it in the bargain." The practical editor of the *Cape May Ocean Wave* urged these improvements "not that we pretend to have more benevolence to the visiting public than others" but rather as a matter of "pocket interest."

Activity increased, as many had predicted. Enterprising people were needed to rejuvenate the war-weary resort, and the railroad acted as a magnet with its promise of fast, comfortable transportation. One such enterprising person was J.F. Cake. He had been the proprietor of the well-respected Willard Hotel in Washington, D.C. He became proprietor of the Columbia Hotel in 1863 and took over the operation of Congress Hall the following year.

In the nineteenth century, a proprietor was traditionally not an owner. He usually leased the hotel for the season, serving more as a manager. A popular proprietor could usually be counted on to bring along a loyal clientele that would follow him from one hotel to another. The importance of a celebrated proprietor is demonstrated by this description of Charles Duffy, who was proprietor of a popular Cape Island hotel seven years later in 1870:

> *Mr. Duffy possesses the essentials of a hotel man. He is fat, he is gentlemanly, and he rarely forgets a face. If you stopped at the Continental Hotel* [Philadelphia] *in 1865 for the first time, and for one day only, and revisited it in 1870, you would be met at the clerk's counter by Mr. Duffy, who would immediately call you by name and warmly welcome you…to flatter a man by making him think he is remembered for five or more years, is to secure his patronage ever afterwards.*

The ads for the hotels always displayed the proprietor's name in a prominent position.

The Summer City by the Sea

As the war came to an end in 1865, the hotel operators prepared for the new season with renewed optimism. The following establishments were open for business for the 1865 season: Congress Hall, Columbia House, the United States Hotel, Atlantic Hotel, Ocean House, Centre House, Washington House, Delaware House, La Pierre House, Metropolitan Hotel, Tremont House, Commercial House, Tontine Hotel, Surf House, Ocean Breeze Hotel, Greenwood Cottage, Cottage by the Sea, Merchants Hotel, Considine Hotel, Continental Hotel, National Hotel and White Hall.

The war had taken a toll on Cape Island. There were some hopes that the wealthy Southerners would return, as illustrated in this newspaper report that described the Grand Promenade Concert and Soiree Dansante, the event that traditionally signaled the start of the summer social season:

> *As we looked upon the crowded room, imagination carried us back to bygone years, when every southern city from Baltimore to New Orleans found its representative upon this self-same floor, and the fervent prayer glided from our lips that soon again all would be united when sober, second thought would re-bring harmony and peace-when bloodshed and strife would be forgotten, and united in dance, the surf, the drive and the geniality of conversation, north and south would be as one.*

These noble sentiments were, understandably, not shared by most of the country. Words like Shiloh, Fredericksburg and Antietam, as well as thoughts of the thousands of men who lost their lives in these bloody battles, were etched in the nation's collective memory.

To add to the problem, many Northerners, including a large Cape May County contingency, believed that the South should be severely punished. The heated Reconstruction debate that rocked the government and eventually led to President Andrew Johnson's impeachment caused a firestorm in Cape May County.

The South was not the answer. Cape Island's future was the railroad. It was now possible for families from Philadelphia and points north to build their own seaside retreat only three and a half hours from the city. War profits had created a new class of visitors and investors. The resort's economy was enhanced as full-time residents recognized the opportunity that parceling their land into lots represented.

The Cottage Era

Widespread belief in the railroad's influence prompted outside investors to back the once regal watering place. One such investor, John C. Bullitt, was to play a major role in the city's postwar expansion. Both an attorney and counsel for the new railroad, Bullitt took advantage of the market the railroad created for both summer cottages and hotel accommodations.

Along with partner Frederick Fairthorne, he acquired the Columbia House in 1864. The two entrepreneurs hired Philadelphia architect Stephen Decatur Button to plan the improvements for the Columbia. Button had recently completed a cottage on the corner of Congress and North Streets for Philadelphian Joseph E. Page. Button's classic style was to have a major influence on the architecture of the island. He created plans for more than thirty buildings in the years that followed the arrival of the railroad.

As the cottage era began in earnest, rival resorts continued to erect hotels, such as the "mammoth hotel being built at Long Branch, New Jersey, which, it is said, will accommodate fifteen hundred guests." The *Cape May Ocean Wave* advised the resort that two similar buildings constructed on the island would be easily filled. This advice probably prompted the construction of the Sherman House, completed in 1866 on the corner of Lafayette and Jackson Streets. The papers were full of reports of numerous cottages under construction on the island and advised readers to "let the cry go forth and re-echo in all our principal cities, that there is room for many more." Areas of the city that "a few years ago were comparative strangers to the footsteps of the visitor" fell under the expansion spell. Bullitt and Fairthorne subdivided the tract opposite their Columbia House in the fall of 1866. The subdivision created Columbia Avenue and Gurney Street.

The February 19, 1868 *Cape May Ocean Wave* noted that the value of the lots created on the new streets, "being situated adjacent to the beach, with an unobstructed view of the ocean, was immediately recognized by several gentlemen of Philadelphia and elsewhere, the lots nearly all sold, and since then some fine cottages were erected."

The article refers to the cottage being erected on Beach Street (later changed to Columbia Avenue) by Peter McCollum, who eventually purchased additional Columbia Avenue lots and constructed "spec" cottages. Two of his cottages were the Oliver Smith house at 705 Columbia and the John Benezet house at 725 Columbia.

Three other cottages that were built on the lots created by the Columbia/Gurney subdivision were the Edward Warne cottage (617 Columbia), the Edward Morris cottage (621 Columbia) and the Samuel Harrison cottage (615 Columbia). The three cottages, designed by Stephen Button, still stand today.

The city government, recognizing the potential for growth that the railroad offered, initiated an aggressive improvement program. New streets such as Grant Street (recently opened by the West Jersey Railroad) offered new locations for summer cottages.

Older streets, including Lafayette and Washington, were widened, improved and extended. Beach Drive was extended, with buildings along the beach being moved or razed during the process. The uniqueness of Cape May's Beach Drive, with no hotels or homes between the ocean strand and the drive, still exists today.

Major hotels in operation during the 1868 season were Congress Hall, the Columbia House, the United States Hotel, the Surf, the Centre House, the Atlantic, the Merchants and the Washington House.

The West Jersey Railroad acquired controlling interest of the Cape May and Millville Railroad in 1868 and consolidated the lines to Philadelphia. A contemporary writer noted, "Each year has added to the excellence of the railroad…cars of the most complete construction and luxurious finish are run, including Woodruff's Silver Palace Drawing Room Coaches…which render the journey of only two hours and a half or less from Philadelphia to the 'City by the Sea' as pleasant as human skill can make it."

The cars kept coming, and the railroad announced plans to construct a large excursion house and hotel on beachfront property that it had purchased between Broadway and Congress Hall. The lot bordered the east end of the footprint where the ill-fated Mount Vernon Hotel had stood. The news caused tremendous excitement throughout the resort since the railroad's plans included operating daily excursion trains during the summer season.

Before the arrival of the railroad, Cape Island had no need for an excursion facility. Tourists who made the full-day journey generally stayed for extended visits. The railroad created a new breed of visitor: the excursionist. Often characterized as "shoobies" because they would carry their lunch in a shoebox, these excursionists were the first genuine day-trippers.

The *Cape May Ocean Wave* reported in its December 18, 1867 issue that "there is no house on the Island that furnished the necessary accommodations and the want has therefore been long experienced by this class of annual visitors." The article described how the hotels' regular boarders expressed a strong "antipathy, perhaps not altogether without cause, for those visitors of a few hours stay—many of whom make it a practice to usurp the privileges of a permanent guest in crowding the parlors, lounging around the doors and offices, bewildering the hotel clerks, promenading the piazzas, and in various other ways occupying space where it is already too limited."

While it seemed that the shoobies were unwanted guests, bringing their own lunch and staying for only a day, the article conceded that "no doubt more or less benefit to the Island is derived from these temporary visitors for the name of the place thus becomes as familiar as a household word in the mouths of thousands who may at some time or other make a much longer stay at the Capes." (The distain the local residents of most New Jersey resorts show for day-trippers is still with us, but the wiser majority realize that those tourist dollars help keep their towns in business.)

The Summer City by the Sea

The major beneficiary of the thousands of shoobies who visited the resort in the nineteenth century was, of course, the railroad, and the new excursion house would profit as well. The frame of the new excursion house was constructed in Camden, New Jersey, and shipped by rail to the site on Grant Street. The railroad had extended its tracks to the beach before the hotel's construction.

Known as the "Sea Breeze," the excursion house was situated within one hundred feet of the ocean and about three hundred feet west of Congress Hall. In July 1868, the building was described by the local paper: "The main building has a front of ninety-one feet, by seventy feet deep and three stories high, with a wing for a dining room, two hundred feet by forty-two feet wide."

There was a general reception room that doubled as a ballroom, drawing rooms for both ladies and gentlemen, washrooms, a kitchen, a laundry and a saloon. The Sea Breeze could comfortably accommodate 1,500 visitors.

The few overnight rooms were reserved for the railroad directors and their guests. Living quarters for employees were provided in a separate building. There were twenty-five-foot-wide verandas surrounding the first and second floor of the main building. The shoobies could entertain themselves playing tenpins on one of the hotel's eight alleys or spending their time in one of the billiard rooms. Bathhouses were a necessity in an era that did not approve of walking the streets in bathing apparel, and the Sea Breeze had more than one hundred conveniently located on the beach.

A "wide plank-walk" that stretched more than one thousand feet was provided "to all who do not desire to walk on the sand." This was a section of the first boardwalk along the Jersey Shore that dates to 1863 in Cape May. The resort is not only the oldest along the New Jersey coastline, but it can also boast the first boardwalk.

Alongside the Sea Breeze was a seven-hundred-foot-long railroad platform. Visitors from Philadelphia could now travel to the resort and disembark almost on the beach, eliminating the inconvenience of hiring a depot hack or wagon to transfer them from the steamboat landing. The Sea Breeze was the finest facility of its kind at the time.

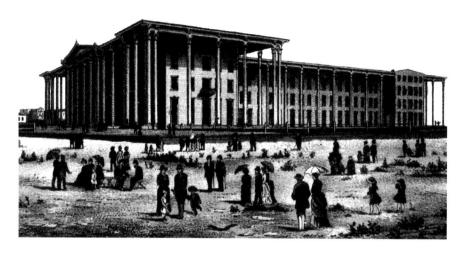

The West Jersey Railroad constructed the Stockton Hotel in 1869 at a cost of more than $300,000. The city of Cape Island altered its charter and became the city of Cape May during the same year. The mammoth Stockton could accommodate more than 475 guests. *Helenclare Leary.*

The railroad next sought to encourage more cottagers by offering the "improvement ticket," or free passage, between Philadelphia and Cape May, to the head of a family building a cottage on Cape Island. The promotion stipulated that the cottage's construction cost, excluding the lot, must exceed $2,500. Many took advantage of the offer, and new cottages continued to fill the resort.

At the end of the 1868 summer season, the railroad announced plans to build a grand hotel on the island that would complement its excursion house, which did not offer overnight rooms. The construction of the giant structure was to be designed by Stephen Decatur Button and supervised by John C. Bullitt and West Jersey Railroad director William Sewell. The estimated cost of the hotel was $300,000, serious money in 1868.

The marshland between Gurney Street, Columbia Avenue and the ocean was filled in to accommodate the massive structure that would be the pride of the city of Cape May. (The city of Cape Island was renamed the city of Cape May by an amendment to the resort's charter in 1869.)

The March 10, 1869 *Cape May Ocean Wave* carried news of the new railroad hotel, the Stockton House, as it was to be named. Each week's paper made mention of the progress: "Just think of it! Upwards of

25,000 lbs. of iron are required to hang the almost innumerable windows of the mammoth Stockton House"…"It takes between three and four thousand dollars every week to pay off the mechanics at work on the Stockton House."

The hotel opened on June 24, 1869, in time for the summer season. Senator Stockton addressed the guests at the inaugural dinner and thanked the railroad for naming the hotel after his deceased father, Commodore Robert Stockton. The new hotel boasted 475 guest rooms and a dining hall that could accommodate eight hundred persons.

The *Cape May Ocean Wave* reported, "By the time dinner and speeches were fairly over, the evening train from Philadelphia arrived, when guests crowded in, filling an extra page of the register with names of permanent boarders, and these have continued to daily increase ever since."

Railroad Control

The new railroad connection, along with the construction of the Sea Breeze excursion house and the Stockton Hotel, signaled to wary investors that the reports of Cape May's demise had been greatly exaggerated.

The papers reported, "[L]ike a butterfly which has just cast off the caterpillar, the Cape Island of 1868 has taken wings and is now putting on airs as the City of Cape May."

The city now had a board of commissioners (à la New York City), a uniformed police force, a new gas company and a racecourse and was now ready to take on Saratoga, Newport and Long Branch as viable vacation spots. Cape May had clearly lost business to Long Branch and the upstart resort of Atlantic City, and it hoped that the railroad would bring a steady flow of New Yorkers to the resort. The papers courted New Yorkers and promised "hotels fit for New Yorkers," further noting that "New York is rich enough to run both places [Cape May and Long Branch]."

During the mid-nineteenth century, Cape May supported two newspapers. The *Cape May Ocean Wave*, established in 1854 by Colonel Johnson, was an important voice for the community. Its motto was "A family journal—Independent in all things, neutral in none." The newspaper was purchased by Joseph S. Leach three months after its founding and then during the Civil War by Samuel Magonagle, who was

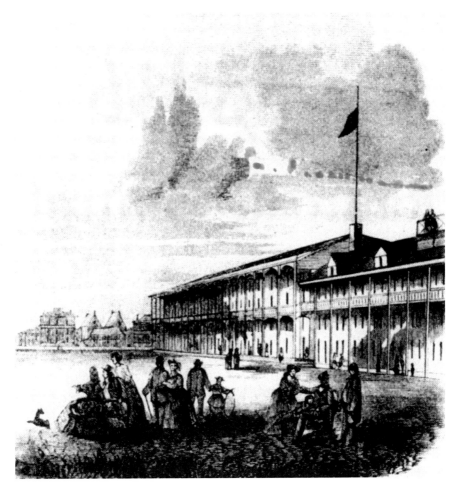

Congress Hall as it looked in the summer of 1859. The main house of the hotel was rebuilt in 1854. The new facility could accommodate more than five hundred guests. *Author's collection.*

later elected mayor of Cape May. As early as 1865, Magonagle published it as a daily in the summer season. The paper's name was changed in the 1870s to the *Cape May Wave*.

The *Star of the Cape* was founded in 1868 at Cape May Court House, New Jersey, and later moved to the city of Cape May. The *Star of the Cape* and the *Cape May Wave*, bitter rivals, were merged in 1907 as the *Star and Wave*. It is thought by many to be the oldest shore resort paper in the United States.

The city's renaissance was summed up by a local editorial: "The secret of this awakening from the Rip Van Winkle under which Cape May has labored so long is that the control of the property and affairs of the island has passed out of the hands of the old fogies who came so near blasting it, and now capital, skill and New York enterprise have taken charge of it. It is now but three hours from Philadelphia and seven from New York." The editor proceeded to assure the citizens that "the brains and skill and enterprise that had the pluck to invest a half million dollars in the Stockton House and its surrounding grounds will take care that their interests do not suffer for want of rapid means of communications with the communities whose patronage is desired." The message was clear: Cape May's future was now in the hands of the railroad.

The West Jersey Railroad improvement ticket proved successful, with fifty cottages being erected between the 1868 and the 1869 seasons.

Local newspaper advertisements offered scores of building lots for sale. The city was illuminated by gas, and the *Cape May Ocean Wave* ran a full-column article titled, "How to Read a Gas Meter," advising hotel owners, shopkeepers and cottagers that "[a] few minutes' practice at reading meters, generally called 'taking a meter,' will make anyone quite familiar with the matter, and will give the gas consumer a wonderful degree of satisfaction, and often bring about a much better feeling toward the gas company."

The existing hotels improved their buildings in order to compete with the new railroad hotels. Congress Hall announced plans to add a new wing along Perry Street. The Columbia House removed its second-floor porches and rebuilt the first-floor porches while also adding a new kitchen to the hotel. Smaller hotels, such as Reigel's New Cottage on Ocean Street and Proskauer's Maison Dorce, located on the corner of Washington and Jackson, were completed and assisted in filling the need for accommodations.

The summer season of 1869 was hailed as the resort's most successful to date. The war had been over for four years, and the railroad transported ocean lovers to Cape May by the thousands.

Baseball became a popular pastime. By the 1869 vacation season, the sport was already twenty-five years old, and its popularity had grown tremendously during the Civil War. Soldiers from Northern urban centers in New York and New Jersey helped spread the game to both sides of the conflict during the long, frequent breaks in fighting. After the war, visiting teams would play while vacationing at Cape May, and before long, the Cape Island Base Ball Club was organized. The club's exhibition games against visiting teams and hotel guests became major summer attractions. Many collegiate stars spent their summers playing for various resort teams. Summer resort baseball maintained its popularity in Cape May well into the twentieth century.

The Fire of 1869

At 2:30 a.m. on August 31, 1869, the summer city by the sea felt what the local reporters referred to as the "breath of the dread Fire-King."

The fire began on Washington Street, between Ocean and Decatur Streets, in a small Oriental goods shop owned by a local character named Peter Paul Boyton, who was known in the city as the "Pearl Diver." He had come by the nickname by acting as sort of a lifeguard for hire. Since there was no organized lifeguard service as yet and drownings were not uncommon, a strong, young swimmer like Boyton could earn money by receiving rewards from sea-bathers he rescued. He was credited with saving more than seventy people over the years.

The *Philadelphia Sunday Dispatch* later reported that "from the little store the red flames embraced the dried and seasoned timbers of the states hotel [United States Hotel]. In an instant its broad proportions became a vast illumination."

The city's single hook and ladder proved useless as the flames spread. Several small cottages and shops were destroyed, and "then in sheer wantonness, the fiend made a flank movement, and, blowing his heated breath across a long stretch of greensward, made a mass of blackened ruin out of the Atlantic hotel."

The Columbia Hotel was preparing itself for the worst. Buckets of water from the hotel's artesian well were used to wet down the old wooden hotel. Just as the building was about to succumb to the flames,

The Summer City by the Sea

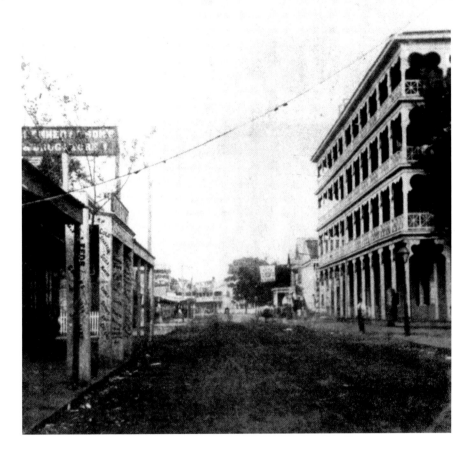

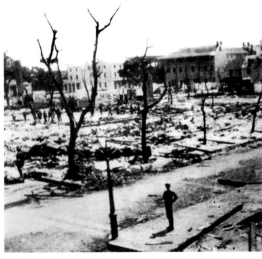

This page: The United States Hotel (above, right) was lost in the 1869 fire. Constructed in 1851, it had been the site of suspicious fires dating back to 1862. The "States," as it was known, was never replaced. The 1869 fire (right) destroyed two blocks that contained the oldest section of the resort. *Cape May County Historical Society.*

fate smiled on the city. The wind shifted and drove the fire back on the destroyed area, where it eventually burned itself out.

With the exception of the Columbia Hotel, everything in the area surrounded by the beach, Washington Street, Ocean Street and Jackson Street was lost. Many of the buildings that composed old Cape Island perished in the fire. The United States Hotel, the New Atlantic and the American Hotel were completely destroyed. Several commercial buildings on Jackson Street, along with numerous cottages and boardinghouses, fell victim to the "Fire-King."

The United States Hotel, built in 1851, represented the most significant loss to the resort. A Philadelphia paper reminisced about the hotel in an article written one year after the fire:

> *It was the first house of any magnitude visible from the car-windows as the train emerged from the woods preparatory to crossing the salt marsh. Its many-storied balconies, its white cupola, and its ever-flying flag were all cheerful, old time landmarks….Many times in the late evening, while the music was wafted from all parts of the Island, have I seated myself on the cool porch, and, while smoking my cigar, I have watched the gay couples pass to and fro from the hotels…and, in fact have felt more comfortable all over than elsewhere.*

The United States Hotel had been the site of suspicious fires dating back to 1862, when the city offered a reward for the apprehension of suspected arsonists. The fire of 1869 was thought by many to have been deliberately set. Peter Boyton was questioned but was later released. In an unrelated incident, Boyton was arrested one month later for firing a pistol from a train window and endangering the life of a local woman, the bullet passing through a door a few inches from her head. He was fined five dollars and released when it was determined that he was "not actuated by malicious motives." He left Cape May shortly after this incident to continue his diving career in other parts of the globe. Whether the cause of the fire was Boyton, the work of an unknown arsonist or merely an accident will never be known. Boyton's experiences in Cape May appear to have been an anomaly since he went on to fame and fortune and became known for his long-distance swimming prowess. He traversed the Irish Sea, the Straits of Gibraltar and the English Channel wearing a pneumatic swimsuit that he invented. The United States Coast Guard used Boyton's suit in the early twentieth century. He opened Boyton's Sea Lion Park in Coney Island in 1895, the first enclosed amusement park ever built.

The fire reduced to ashes two blocks of the oldest section of the resort. The papers editorialized about "carelessness and neglect of precautionary measures," but the editors knew that the wooden cities of their era burned often; they later lamented that "there is no getting behind the fact, fires have and do take place here and elsewhere with as much regularity as if they sprang from the evolution of some natural law."

The United States Hotel was never rebuilt. The land where the building stood was auctioned and subdivided into lots. The aging New Atlantic Hotel that was lost in the blaze was the only hotel rebuilt after the fire. Plans were announced to build a hotel on the site of the old one for a cost of about $100,000. It was to be completed by the summer of 1870.

Depression and Reconstruction

The railroad continued to drive the boom, and it would take more than a two-city-block fire to slow it down. Cape May was fast becoming a city that was owned by outside cottagers and investors. Most of the residents were pleased with the railroad expansion and saw no end to the boom. The West Jersey Railroad gained more and more control of the "island," as regular visitors referred to the resort.

A newspaper article in June 1870 reported, "The West Jersey Railroad Company and a number of gentlemen associated with it have contributed largely towards our up-building, and the indications are that they will more extensively in the future. To the Board of Commissioners, created by special act of the Legislature, much is also owing."

This story referred to a special commission that was appointed by the state legislature, completely independent of the duly elected city council. The commission represented the railroad's interest, and the city's "improvements" were now in its hands.

Citizen support for the commission was so strong that a special election engineered by the city council in 1872 to oust the commission had the opposite result. The commission was retained, and at the next regular election, two council members who had opposed the commission lost their bid for reelection and were replaced by commission supporters. The commission was the architect of Cape May's growth until it was finally abolished in 1875, when the city's charter was revised.

The Summer City by the Sea

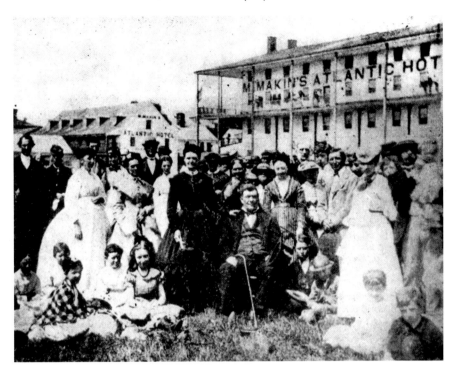

McMakin's Atlantic Hotel, taken before the 1869 fire that destroyed it. John McMakin rebuilt the New Atlantic Hall and operated it on "strict temperance principles." *Federal Writers' Project (WPA), 1937–38.*

As the summer season of 1870 began, the building and improvements continued. The new season was assisted by an early June heat wave, with Philadelphia reporting temperatures of ninety-eight degrees in the shade.

As promised, the New Atlantic was completed on the site of the original lost in the 1869 fire. The proprietor, John McMakin, had taken possession of the old Atlantic two months before the fire. "In one single night his entire fortune was swept away by the breath of the dread Fire-King," the *Cape May Ocean Wave* reported. "The earnings of a life-time were buried in the ashes; but he stood it manfully."

His New Atlantic was four stories high and commanded a fine view of the ocean. All of its rooms were lit by gas, and the new structure could accommodate two hundred guests at one time. McMakin operated his hotel on "strict temperance principles."

Scores of commercial and residential structures opened for the new season. Washington Street alone was the site of more than twenty-five new cottages and stores. Congress Hall invested $250,000 on a new wing and bragged of having more than 150 rooms booked at the beginning of the season.

The grandest private residence opening for the 1870 season was the Senator John B. McCreary "marine residence," built in 1869 at a cost of $20,000. The structure was designed by architect Stephen Decatur Button. Its location on the corner of Columbia Avenue and Gurney Street validated John Bullitt's theory that his Stockton Hotel would attract the best class of cottagers. The improvements made to Beach Drive allowed carriages easier access to the east side and the Stockton area. The McCreary residence still stands today and is a popular bed-and-breakfast guesthouse.

The newspapers officially declared the opening of the 1870 season: "We are now ready for the reception of guests. All the hotels are open… and the crowds of swells and diversified fashionables in all colors of silks, ribbons and things, are beginning to pour down upon us." The article added, "[T]he fact is daily becoming more and more apparent to capitalists that no better or safer investments can be found than by converting their stocks into Cape May property."

The railroad economy remained strong. The following year, 1870–71, eight Stockton Row cottages were constructed on Gurney Street in the shadow of the massive Stockton House. The year 1872 witnessed the construction of Jackson's Clubhouse on Columbia Avenue at the corner of Howard Street. Originally built as a gambling house, the building exists today as a charming bed-and-breakfast.

It finally took the economy to do what the fire of 1869 could not. The Cape May railroad boom came to a screeching halt in 1873 when a financial panic, brought on by the failure of several important eastern banks, caused a nationwide depression. Funds for new construction and major improvements disappeared almost overnight, and the resort experienced a downturn that surpassed the lean Civil War years in severity.

Many families witnessed their dreams of a summer cottage by the sea vanish as the depression gripped the economy for five long years. Hundreds of cottages and lots were sold at auction by the city for unpaid taxes. One enterprising storekeeper ran advertisements offering rings, pins and studs made with genuine Cape May diamonds at prices "to suit the times."

No major structures were erected during the depression, although some small buildings were built. In 1875, local Civil War hero Henry Sawyer constructed the Chalfonte on Howard Street, which is still in operation today.

As the depression began to show signs of weakening in 1876, investors took another look at Cape May. The West Jersey Railroad had previously improved its excursion house site by adding a small summer station. The success of the station was such that a larger structure, known as the Grant Street Summer Station, was built in 1876 at a cost of $20,000. (The winter station was located at the intersection of Jackson and Lafayette Streets.)

After the America's Cup was successfully defended in 1876, Cape May immediately caught yachting fever. (The yacht *Madeline* twice defeated the Canadian challenger *Countess of Dufferin*.)

The city invited yachting clubs from New York, Baltimore and Philadelphia to participate in a Grand Regatta. To accommodate the yachtsmen, proprietor of Congress Hall J.F. Cake constructed a pier. A contemporary description of the enterprise noted that "a convenient wharf has been constructed immediately in front of Congress Hall lawn, for the accommodation of these pleasure crafts, whose American owners have won honorable laurels in many lands."

Vacationers could now board the express train between Philadelphia and Cape May and arrive in less than three hours. A regular ticket cost $2.50, and the family servant could make the trip for $2.00. A season ticket, good between June 1 and October 1, was priced at $50.00.

Cape May, along with Atlantic City, experienced competition for tourist dollars from Philadelphia, the location of the Centennial Exposition, a world's fair in honor of the country's 100th birthday in 1876. The exposition began in May and ended in November, attracting more than 10 million sojourners to the Quaker City. (The Philadelphia Centennial Committee visited Atlantic City during the same year, signaling organizations around the country that the newer resort was the place to hold their next convention. This rebuff to Cape May, by its patron city, was an indication that the older resort was slowly losing the battle with its neighbor to the north.)

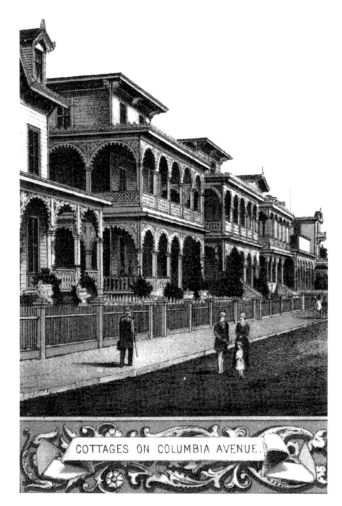

The Columbia Avenue cottages were constructed as a result of the Stockton Hotel, which opened in 1869. The massive hotel occupied the entire block between Howard and Gurney Streets and Columbia Avenue and the ocean. *Helenclare Leary.*

The railroad had a substantial investment in Cape May and published lavish brochures promoting the seaside city. One such booklet printed in 1876 provided a detailed description of the city's beachfront:

> *The Stockton House is the easternmost and right-hand house in the picture. Next is seen the Columbia House, hemmed in by lines of tasteful cottages and bathhouses, and fronted by a wide, grassy lawn. Next to the left, at the corner of the street, comes the cubical bulk of*

the Atlantic, a serviceable, free-and-hearty house, notable for being open all year round. To the left of the Atlantic is seen the long facade of Congress Hall, a house able to entertain two thousand guests. Quite at the edge of the picture, and the last large structure represented this side of the lighthouse, is the Sea Breeze Hotel, the great wholesale depot of the excursion parties...Such is the chain of first-class houses fronting immediately on the sea, to which must be added the Ocean House, the Chalfonte, the Centre, the Arctic, the Merchants, the National, the St. Charles, the United States [the Sherman House was leased by Aaron Miller in 1870 and renamed the United States; the hotel of the same name lost in the 1869 fire was never rebuilt], *and a crowd of respectable select establishments merging insensibly into boarding house.*

This was the resort of Cape May in 1876. By 1878, it seemed that Cape May might again begin to experience a period of growth. An expanding national economy promised more investments and improvements that were severely needed to help the venerable resort compete with Long Branch and Atlantic City.

A severe yellow fever epidemic that would eventually claim more than fourteen thousand lives sent anyone who could afford it running from the cities to the country or the seaside. Many sought the often-

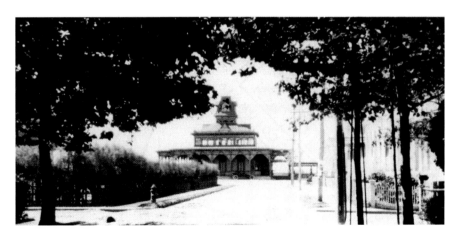

The Grant Street Summer Station was constructed by the West Jersey Railroad in 1876 at a cost of $20,000. *H. Gerald MacDonald.*

promised healthful benefits of the sea. Cape May advertised "the multitudes who have here escaped the reeking atmosphere of crowded cities or the dusty days and sultry nights of the country; who have felt the genial influences of the Cape dispel their mental weariness or convert in some magic way a train of morbid fancies into healthy intellectual vigor, will fail to recall the lack of any desideratum amongst those in the repertoire which Cape May offers so generously to its guests."

Whether to escape disease or just enjoy a "summer loiter," the sea lovers began to fill the hotels and boardinghouses at the beginning of the 1878 summer season. When the trains arrived, dozens of hotel coaches greeted passengers as they stepped onto the depot platform. Confusion reigned as the coach drivers endeavored to outshout one another and the steam locomotive, calling out the names of the hotels that had hired them to pick up boarders who arrived both with and without reservations.

Mixed in among the wagons were a hundred or more people, some attempting to meet a friend or relative arriving on the train and some just passing the time watching the commotion. The sound of the surf, just a

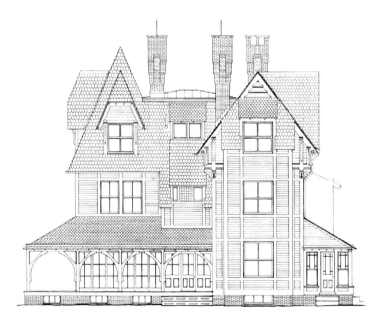

The Emlen Physick House, constructed in 1878–79, played a major role in Cape May's survival almost a century later. The structure is believed to have been designed by Frank Furness. *Historic American Buildings Survey.*

hundred feet from the station, accompanied the symphony of train, man and beast that repeated itself with each new trainload of excursionists.

Those who preferred a more gracious means of travel followed with anticipation the progress of the new grand steamer that was under construction at Wilmington, Delaware, as the summer season began. The three-deck vessel, the *Republic*, would soon be capable of completing the trip from Philadelphia to Cape May in five and a half leisurely hours, including a stop at New Castle.

The railroad terminus was beginning to attract development on the west side of the resort. The Arlington Hotel was constructed for John Kromer of Baltimore on Grant Street near the summer train station. The *Star of the Cape* reported in August that a grand cottage was to be built in another section of town: "Mrs. Ralston's new cottage will be… designed in the English style of architecture, and will be entirely different from any other cottage here." Mrs. Ralston was Emlen Physick's mother, and the article referred to what is known today as the Physick House. The architect is believed to have been Philadelphian and Cape May cottager Frank Furness.

The August 3, 1878 edition of the *Cape May Ocean Wave* advised the community that "the city has done well of late, but the impression must not obtain that all is done." The editorial went on to call for the construction of an iron ocean pier that could accommodate steamboats and recreational vessels. (In 1878, Cape May had two wooden piers: the Congress Hall pier and the Denizot pier.) The editor suggested that should the pier be constructed, "prominent New Yorkers that much travel from that city to Cape May would ensue, bringing patronage that is now lost to us, but which is carried to other resorts of inferior attraction."

The 1878 season was said to be the most successful ever. The editor of the *Cape May Wave* cautioned the residents of the island that "we have achieved a triumph the present season which augurs well for the future, but there are lessons taught by this achievement which must not be unheeded or unstudied."

As the hotels boarded shut their windows and doors for the long winter and the city anticipated its annual hibernation, the *Cape May Wave* commented on the end of the season:

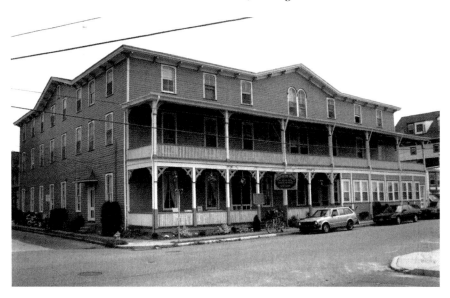

The West Jersey Railroad's construction of the Grant Street Summer Station promoted growth on the west side of the city. The Arlington House (seen here), built on Grant Street in the vicinity of the station in 1878, is one of the oldest surviving hotels in Cape May. *Photo by Emil R. Salvini.*

> *All who still remain at Cape May and those who continue to make it the objective point of their flying trips from the city, find a change in its summer life of a few days so complete and sudden as to seem almost magical. The great hotels, and a number of the smaller ones, which were but lately the scene of so much gaiety and animated human life now look silent and deserted, with their closed doors and shutters, as if a human foot had never crossed their thresholds, and long rows and groups of cottages, too, with here and there an exception, are wrapped in the profound silence which succeeds the close of the season.*

Fate was about to break the "profound silence" of the summer city by the sea, and nothing would ever be the same again.

The Inferno

The old Ocean House on Perry Street across from Congress Hall was situated on a precious piece of real estate, only half a block from the beach and close to most of Cape May's notable cottages and hotels. Sometime during the early hours of November 9, 1878, while the city slept, one or more arsonists entered the vacant hotel, which had closed for the winter.

The fire was first observed by a roofer, repairing the Stockton Hotel, at about 7:00 a.m. Although he noticed smoke emitting from the roof, no alarm was sounded until a few minutes later when, as the papers would later report, "a lady standing at the corner of Washington Street was remarked by Colonel Sawyer, a member of city council, to be gazing intently in the direction of the Ocean House." A general alarm was sounded, and the ringing of the city's church bells alerted the sleepy citizens that the fire fiend was afoot.

The old resort was easy prey. An editorial would later lament, "Vast towering hotels, of the most combustible wood, narrow streets, a location where strong winds are the rule, and the absence of anything like an adequate fire service—Here were the elements essential to disastrous fire."

Shortly after the alarm was sounded, flames burst through the Ocean House roof in half a dozen places. A thirty-six-mile-per-hour northwest wind fanned the flames, and it soon became apparent that the old hotel was lost.

Excited residents began to wonder if the inadequate fire department could stop the fiend from claiming the surrounding properties. The local firefighting equipment consisted of an "antiquated hand engine, with fifteen hundred feet of rubber hose, three small chemical engines and a hook-and-ladder truck." The authorities, sensing the severity of the situation, sent word to Camden for a steamer and additional hose.

The heat generated from the well-seasoned timbers of the Ocean House soon ignited the new wing of Congress Hall on the opposite side of Perry Street. A reporter would later note that "all that was needed to save Congress Hall…was a little water. All the hose was in use, and several precious moments were lost before the necessary connection could be made to bring the hand-engine into play, which prior to this time had been standing idle."

As Congress Hall burned, the fire spread from the Ocean House to the Merchants Hotel Complex. The Merchants was actually two three-story buildings, located midway between the Atlantic Hotel and the Centre House on Jackson Street, immediately adjoining the Ocean House property. (The Continental had been joined with the Merchants in 1866 to form one hotel.)

A citizen bucket brigade, along with two streams of precious water from the Jackson Street fire-plug, gave the firefighters hope that they had checked the fire's advance on Jackson Street. The supply of fire hose was inadequate and in shabby condition.

The *Cape May Wave* later reported that "there were still hopes that the hotel [Congress Hall] would be saved, and the strong probability is that with a moderate supply of water it would, but for the unfortunate bursting of the hose just as the engine had got fairly started." Five additional sections of hose were brought into service, and each burst within minutes. As the valiant firefighters struggled with the equipment, Congress Hall gave up the ghost and succumbed to the conflagration. A witness later described the eerie scene: "Congress Hall as it burned presented a magnificent scene from the beach front, the flames pouring out from its hundred windows, enveloping balconies and verandahs, leaping into the air a hundred feet, and making a noise like the thundering of a score of express trains over a wooden bridge."

The immense lawn of the mammoth hotel took on the appearance of an auction as furniture from the first-floor rooms was carried from the inferno in an effort to save it. Most was lost to looters or quickly transformed to ashes as showers of embers rained from the hotel.

The flames next claimed the Fryer cottage, located between the Ocean House and the beach, and quickly reduced the outbuildings on the Ocean House property to rubble. Still ravenous, the fire fiend traveled to the corner of Perry and Washington Streets and devoured the Centre House. Hope blossomed again as the firefighters heard the beautiful sound of the steam locomotive whistle, announcing the arrival of the steamer from Camden.

The frightened crowd continued to look on as rows and rows of cottages and boardinghouses perished. A reporter later described the community's fear at that moment:

Nothing could have been more arbitrary than the progress of the hungry, destroying power, which lashed itself, now sinuously downward, underlapping eaves and portico roofs with a whirring, puffing noise, like some mighty creature of life, and now shooting upwards with a force and suddenness that cleared roofs and all like a flash, and stood erect, livid and gleaming in the air, as though threatening the very dome of heaven.

The Atlantic Hotel, built after the fire of 1869 had devoured its namesake, quickly fell victim to the inferno, along with its hundreds of beachfront bathhouses.

As was the case in any wooden city, each building passed on the fatal flames to its next-door neighbor. The fire jumped across Jackson Street from the Atlantic Hotel and claimed the row of buildings on the east side of Jackson, including the Knickerbocker Hotel and the Excelsior Hot and Cold Baths. Next to fall was Denizot's Sea View cottage, located on Decatur Street, along with part of its ocean pier.

The Weightman block of commercial buildings stood on the corner of Perry and Washington Streets. The firefighters knew that if this corner fell to the hungry beast, the essential commercial district of Washington Street would succumb. They had nearly exhausted themselves emptying the buildings of all contents and directing as much water on the site as their equally exhausted equipment would allow, when the spectators' cheers signaled to all that the Camden steamer

Historic Cape May, New Jersey

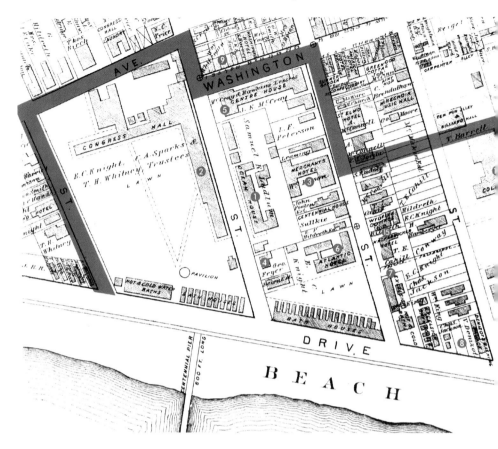

The outlined section of the map indicates the area of the city destroyed by the fire. *Fire progress map created by Emil R. Salvini.*

1. The fire began in the Ocean House, located on Perry Street.
2. Congress Hall was lost when flames from the Ocean House ignited its Perry Street wing.
3. The fire spread from the Ocean House to the Merchants Hotel, which was located behind the Ocean House, fronting on Jackson Street.
4. Flames from the Ocean House claimed another neighbor, Fryer Cottage, located on Perry Street.
5. One of Cape May's oldest hotels, the Centre House, was the fifth victim of the blaze.
6. As the Centre House burned, the fire traveled from the Fryer Cottage to the Atlantic Hotel, which had been rebuilt after the fire of 1869. The hotel and bathhouses were lost.
7. The fire crossed Jackson Street and destroyed the Knickerbocker Hotel and the Excelsior Hot and Cold Baths.
8. The fire spread from Jackson Street to Decatur Street via Denizot's Sea View Cottage.
9. The Weightman block of commercial buildings and the Washington Avenue commercial district were saved by the arrival of more efficient firefighting equipment from Camden, New Jersey.
10. The fire reached the mammoth Columbia House via King's Cottage.
11. The survival of Warne's Drugstore was seen as the key to preventing the fire's spread to the mighty Stockton Hotel. The tiny structure was saved and still stands today.

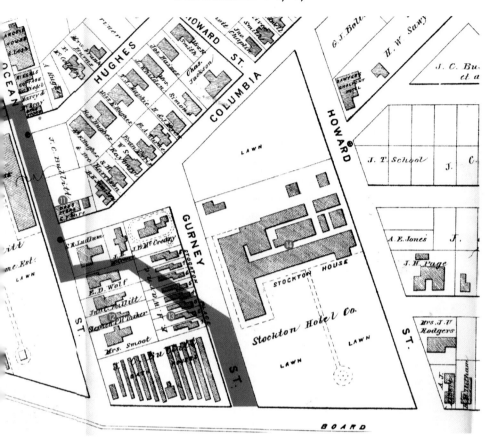

12. The Ocean Street cottages were lost and in turn ignited the Stockton Row cottages that fronted on Gurney Street.
13. The Stockton Row cottages sustained minor damage but were saved by firefighters and still stand today.
14. The Stockton Hotel survived the fire with no damage.
15. The Wyoming House stables, located in the center of the conflagration and full of dry straw, miraculously survived the blaze.

had been unloaded from the train. The equipment was immediately put into service, and a deluge of welcome water saved the corner and the district from imminent destruction. Along with the new steamer came Camden's Chief Bradshaw, who took control of the battle. Up to this time, the locals had been working without a central command.

Many historians would later incorrectly deduce that the disaster could have been prevented if the city had had an ample supply of water. The facts do not support this theory. Though there was plenty of water, there was no way to efficiently direct it where it was needed. Several of the hotels had their own artesian wells but had disconnected the pumps at the end of the season to prevent winter damage.

The *Cape May Wave* later reported that "[l]uckily the city's supply of water was ample for the emergency. The large surface well, 25 feet in diameter and 30 feet deep, was full beside the two elevated tanks, which had a capacity of 90,000 gallons, fed from an inexhaustible artesian well. So well did this source of supply hold out that it was not till the fire had been checked at five o'clock in the afternoon that it began to weaken."

As the Camden steamer attempted to soak several of the burning buildings along Jackson Street, the blaze seemed at last to be under control. The firefighters and crowds expected that the battle would soon be over when the devastating news reached them: the fire had reached the Columbia House, located between Decatur and Ocean Streets. The three-story building was constructed in the classic seaside "L" shape, with each wing more than 180 feet in length. One of the city's best-known hotels, the Columbia could accommodate more than six hundred guests. A massive lawn separated the hotel from the beach, with 275 bathhouses built along the strand. Two three-story cottages were located on the lawn, between the hotel and the ocean.

The fire reached the two cottages via the King's cottages on Decatur Street. The Columbia House was attacked from a different front. A witness later noted:

> *The nearest point of the fire to the windward of the Columbia House was the Centre House, with two solidly built blocks of buildings intervening. From Jackson Street to Ocean the fire sailed over the most densely built portion of the Island as directly as an arrow following the course of the wind, and, leaving stores, the Opera House and other buildings untouched, planted itself on the southern edge of the Ocean Street wing of the old Columbia. In ten minutes the flames were beyond control.*

The fire seemed to have a mind of its own, and panic spread through the crowds. The control center sent word to Camden: "Send Another Steamer…Immediately."

The Summer City by the Sea

As the venerable Columbia Hotel burned into history, a nightmarish idea began to take form: could the fire reach the massive Stockton Hotel? Its loss in the face of the day's destruction would be disastrous to the island. The last line of defense separating the Stockton from the blaze were the eight Stockton Row cottages on Gurney Street and the row of Ocean Street cottages between Columbia Avenue and the sea.

Flames from the Columbia spread northward, destroying the hotel's outbuildings and Barrett's tenpin alley and shooting gallery. Six weary citizens connected a section of discarded hose to the fire-plug on the corner of Washington and Ocean Streets and successfully halted the fire's northward advance.

The survival of Warne's Drugstore, on the opposite side of Ocean Street, at its junction with Columbia Avenue, became imperative. The small structure was scorched, but it still stood (and still does today though not as a drugstore).

A spectator later wrote, "The Stockton, Columbia Avenue and properties east seemed doomed…The fight for its [Warne's] safety was of the most desperate order, because on its preservation really depended the existence of the last of our large hotels, the Stockton, and surrounding properties."

The Camden steamer was moved from Washington Street to the intersection of Columbia Avenue and Gurney Street. In the meantime, the Ocean Street cottages south of Columbia Avenue had ignited and were beyond hope. Seven hundred of the Stockton's bathhouses located along Beach Drive, from Ocean to Gurney Streets, were reduced to ashes. The Wolf cottage on Ocean Street was the fire's last victim. Ironically, the Ludlam cottage, belonging to Ocean House proprietor Samuel Ludlam and located within ten feet of the Wolf cottage, was spared.

Several of the Stockton Row cottages ignited, but thanks to several "plucky firemen," they were saved and still stand today. The mighty Stockton Hotel was saved. By the time the second Camden steamer arrived, at about 4:30 p.m., the fire was declared under control. Washington Street was saved.

As night fell, the steady northwest breeze that had spread the fury during the day continued to fan the red-hot coals into small fires that, from a distance, gave the appearance of a vast military campsite. The moon shone with unusual brilliance, illuminating the acres of wreckage. The fire smoldered for days, and the railroad was forced to assign special trains into service to accommodate the hundreds of curiosity seekers who wished to see the site. Most were shocked at the severity of the destruction. One witness reported that not one cord of wood was left in the "burnt district," as the fire site became known. The heart of Cape May had vanished in one day. (The report that not one cord of wood survived the holocaust was not entirely accurate. A curious side note to the fire was that the stables of the Wyoming House, located on Jackson Street opposite the Atlantic Hotel, filled with dry straw and in the middle of the conflagration, escaped completely intact.)

Newspapers throughout the country began to carry reports of the fire to every corner of the United States. The local *Cape May Wave* announced:

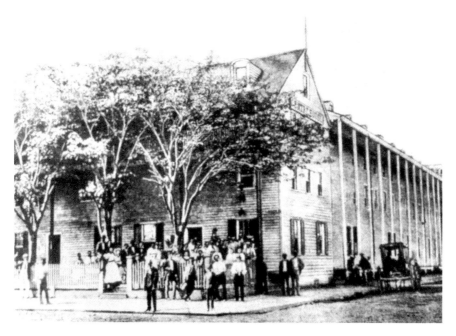

The Centre House, constructed in 1840, was completely destroyed by the fire. It was located between Perry and Jackson Streets, fronting on Washington Street. *Cape May County Historical Society.*

The Summer City by the Sea

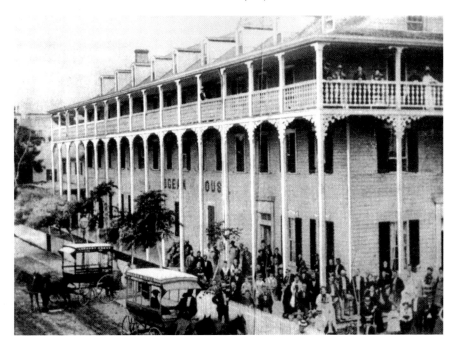

The Ocean House was located on Perry Street. The pre–Civil War hotel was the site of the origin of the 1878 fire, believed to be caused by arson. *Cape May County Historical Society.*

CAPE MAY'S GREATEST FIRE
Thirty-Five Acres of Devastation and Ruins

Seven hotels were lost: Congress Hall, The Columbia, The Ocean House, The Centre House, The Atlantic, The Merchants and The Avenue.

More than thirty cottages and boarding houses were destroyed, along with two thousand bathhouses. The major urban papers attempted to affix blame. It became obvious that regardless of the origin of the blaze, the City of Cape May had been totally unprepared to combat a major fire.

The *Philadelphia Evening Bulletin* reported:

The fate of a wooden town which has inferior fire engines and few of them, and which equips its fire department with cheap hose, is certain destruction sooner or later. It is simply pitiable that there should have been complaint of an insufficient supply of water with the Atlantic Ocean but a stone's throw from the burning buildings.

The *Philadelphia Daily Times* noted:

Its origin, a subject, naturally, of most determined questioning. That flames should break out suddenly in the upper part of an uninhabited hotel is not so commonplace an occurrence that it can be passed by remark, nor is it possible, in view of the great destruction wrought by the flames, to be satisfied with any of the ordinary hypotheses which fire marshals and kindred officials are in the habit of concealing their ignorance...It need[s] no investigation to discover why the fire spread as it did, and why the feeble efforts to combat it proved ineffective. So highly inflammable a town as Cape May ought to be especially well provided with engines and hose, but Cape May appears to have been scarcely provided for at all and the inhabitants were utterly untrained in the duties of firemen.

They will get little sympathy, but they ought to learn from this that if they expect capitalists to build hotels in their town—and without hotels there would be no town there—they must make some effort for their protection.

The fire department was reorganized in 1879. An 1881 city directory lists its equipment as "one first-class rotary Silsby engine and one first-class hook and ladder truck."

The *Philadelphia Evening Telegraph* reported:

Between now and the opening of the next season it will be possible to rebuild the hotels and cottages, but as to whether it will be worthwhile to rebuild them, there seems to be differences of opinion. Cape May, not a great many years ago, had but few rivals among the seaside resorts and now it has a great many. All along the Jersey coast eligible bits of ground, with fair to middling beachfronts, have been taken up by associations, religious and secular, and converted into wateringplaces, and many of these, either because they are more readily accessible or because of features which have special attractions to

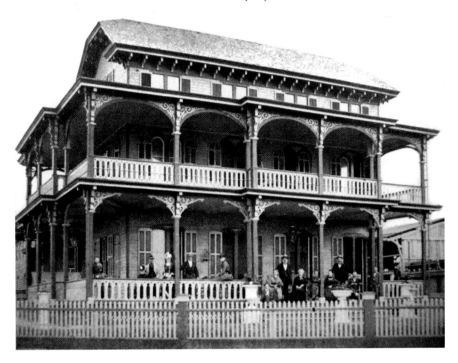

The beautiful King's Cottage was lost in the blaze. *Cape May County Historical Society.*

certain classes of summer loiterers, have drawn away from Cape May a great many of its patrons.

The editorial held out hope for the damaged old resort by reminding readers that Cape May possessed a resource that none of its new competitors could offer: "the beach at Cape May is superb." (These words were written in an era when man had not yet altered the ocean's natural flow and Cape May's world-renowned beachfront was still intact.)

One optimistic statistic was that no life was lost during the terrible fire. On a darker note, though, the local paper reported that as desperate hotel and cottage owners hurried to save their possessions from the inferno, there was an ample supply of scoundrels ready to cart them away. Not unlike the early days when a certain type of individual saw the plight of a grounded ship off the cape as an opportunity to acquire "pickens," many saw the fire as an opportunity to benefit from others' misery. For weeks after the fire, policemen recovered in a variety of places furniture, store goods, clocks and fine linens that were stolen during the catastrophe.

The *Cape May Wave* reported:

> *Goods of every description stolen from the buildings during the fire have since been recovered…On one man's premises four wagon-loads of furniture taken off Congress Hall lawn after the fire were found secreted. The Atlantic Hotel parlor carpet was found in a tank near the lighthouse; boxes of stores from the hotels were recovered in private houses miles from the scene of the disaster; whole suites of chamber furniture were found in actual use in respectable households, and in many instances the issuing of legal processes was necessary to compel the delivery of the stolen property.*

As to the cause of the fire, many were questioned, including the owner of the Ocean House, Samuel R. Ludlam, who it was reported had left Cape May on the early morning train the day of the fire and was not aware that his hotel was destroyed until he reached Millville. The old hotel was insured, and many suspected Ludlam.

The *Cape May Wave* reported on November 27, 1878:

> *The proper affidavit having been filed by one of the sufferers, Mr. Ludlam appeared before the Mayor, and the charge being read, he waived a hearing, when he was required to furnish security in the sum of $2000 to be and appear before the Court of Common Pleas, the third Tuesday in December, to answer to the charge of having set fire to his hotel.*

No concrete proof could be uncovered, and no one was ever convicted of the terrible crime.

The Road Not Taken

A contemporary description of the 1878 pre-fire Cape May skyline, observed from the deck of a passing sailboat, spoke of the "flashing lines of festival lights connecting the continuous row of monstrous four-floored buildings, seeming to touch each other."

These lights were anchored on each end by railroad properties, the Sea Breeze excursion house on the western end of the city and the great Stockton on the east. Although both of these hotels survived the inferno, the "continuous row of monstrous buildings" between them was reduced to ashes.

The impact of this fire differed significantly from the 1869 blaze in two ways. The first was its size; the 1878 fire destroyed a much greater area—more than thirty-five acres. The second major difference was that the earlier blaze occurred in the midst of the railroad economic boom. Plenty of investors were eager to rebuild before the arrival of the next summer season.

The 1878 fire took place at the end of a boom period; the resort and nation were still emerging from the 1873 depression. To make matters worse, Cape May's competitors had grown in number and success, and the Queen of the Seaside Resorts' crown was tarnished.

A rather disingenuous article appeared in an Atlantic City paper immediately after the fire that claimed to sympathize with its neighbor to the south. The reporter said that while many believed that "Cape

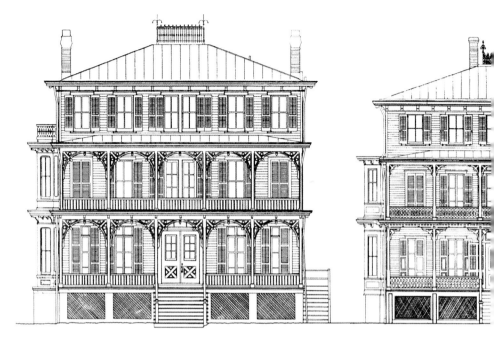

Left to right: E.C. Knight House (1881–82), 203 Congress Place; J.R. Evans House (1881–82), 207 Congress Place; and Dr. Henry F. Hunt House (1881), 209 Congress Place. All three were constructed after the fire of 1878, when Congress Place was cut through the rear of the Congress Hall property. *Historical American Buildings Survey.*

May cannot recover," he was confident that out of the ruins "will arise a handsomer and more modern city" (like Atlantic City), and it "will have the attraction of being new and clean."

The writing was on the wall; Cape May was losing the war for Philadelphia dollars with Atlantic City. A sweltering day in the Quaker City caused so many Philadelphians to seek the relief of Atlantic City that the railroads, in an effort to accommodate the masses, would press into service boxcars with makeshift benches.

Amusement rides such as the Epicycloidal Swing (1879) and later the Ferris wheel (1892) attracted the young in droves. The first Easter Parade was held in Atlantic City on April 16, 1876, and proved an immense success.

Cape May was no longer considered a serious contender of Newport, Rhode Island, for the nation's leisure-class trade. By 1874, there were more than five hundred cottages and villas in the New England resort.

The Summer City by the Sea

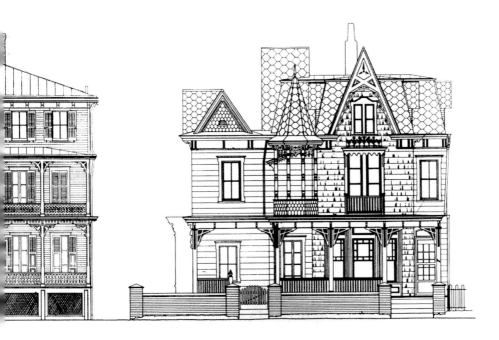

In 1878, the year of the fire, there were as many Philadelphians summering in Newport as in Cape May. By the last two decades of the nineteenth century, the Vanderbilt family had constructed Marble House and the Breakers, Newport "summer cottages" larger than Cape May's best hotels, and the country's new millionaires followed their example. (Before the Civil War there were fewer than a dozen millionaires in the United States. By the end of the nineteenth century, there were more than four thousand.)

A short article in the *Cape May Wave* on December 7, 1878, gave a clue to the direction Cape May was to take after the fire: "Mr. S.D. Button, the able architect of the Stockton House, Mr. J.B. McCreary's cottage, Mrs. Hallenback's villa, and others of our most beautiful buildings, paid us a visit, displaying some superb drawings of hotels which may yet adorn the places made waste by fire. We gladly welcome this ardent friend of Cape May among us once more. His visits have not been frequent of late."

Stephen Decatur Button was sixty-five years old in 1878. He had established himself as a leading architect in the decade preceding the Civil War and had spent several years designing homes for the wealthy in Florida, Georgia and Alabama. Button had won the commission to design the Alabama capitol building in 1847 and produced a building typical of the early American Greek Revival style. He later moved to Philadelphia, where his contacts with the railroad eventually led him to Cape May. Button's first commission in Cape May was to modernize the Columbia House in 1863 for West Jersey Railroad executive John C. Bullitt. During the next decade, he designed numerous cottages and hotels in Cape May, and the wooden summer city by the sea fell in love with his classical style.

By 1878, Stephen Button was no longer in demand by a fashion-conscious leisure class that preferred younger, more progressive architects like Richard Morris Hunt, a favorite of the Vanderbilt family. The fire represented an opportunity for the aging architect. It became immediately clear that, with few exceptions, Cape May would rebuild itself as a smaller, scaled-down version of the pre-fire summer city.

The northern end of the Congress Hall property was subdivided. A new street, Congress Place, was cut through the property, and cottage lots were sold. Congress Hall was rebuilt as a smaller version of the great hotel. Brick was used in its construction to advertise that it was modern and fireproof, but the hotel was constructed in the traditional L-shaped style, which provided an ocean view for the maximum number of rooms. Although Button was not the architect for the new Congress Hall, he was later hired in 1880 to make improvements on the structure.

Button designed the Joseph Evans cottage on one of the new Congress Place lots (205 Congress Place) in his classical style. He received two major commissions: the first to design a new oceanfront hotel, the Windsor, and the second a commission for Victor Denizot's Lafayette Hotel, located at Ocean Street and Beach Drive. The two new hotels that Button designed mimicked the traditional seaside hotel popular thirty years earlier.

Because the majority of cottages built after the fire were constructed without architectural plans, it was common for carpenters to follow the lines of existing cottages or borrow designs from the popular pattern books, collections of Victorian homes of varying costs and styles. In the case of Cape May, most were styled after the simply ornamented, Italianate "Button" style that the resort had fallen in love with decades before the fire.

The property owners of Cape May were presented with a blank canvas after the rubble of the 1878 fire was carted away. Their

The Summer City by the Sea

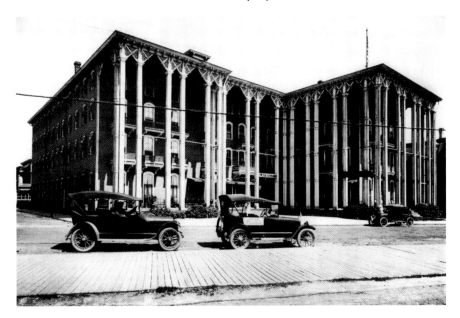

Stephen Decatur Button designed the Lafayette Hotel for Victor Denizot in the traditional L-shaped Cape May style, allowing for the maximum number of rooms with an ocean view. The hotel stood at Ocean Street and Beach Drive. *Library of Congress.*

decision to not attempt to compete with the more popular resorts limited the town's growth, but it fortuitously preserved the intimate character of the town that so many value today.

A popular nineteenth-century poem titled "The Humors of Cape May" spoke of frolicking in the famous Cape May strand, the gently sloping floor of beautiful white sand where the surf breaks. Cape May had been blessed with a strand that was superior to any of its competitors. (It was not until after the turn of the century that man would tamper with nature and unwittingly damage forever the resource around which the city was created.)

Vacationers seeking excitement chose Atlantic City. Those wishing to demonstrate to the world that they had "arrived" traveled to Newport, but the nineteenth-century sojourner in search of a "health-giving" sea-bath still preferred Cape May.

Cape Island had, according to an 1881 Cape May directory, "a rolling surf, safe at all times, and within easy access from the shore and the boardinghouses," with numerous piers that afforded "a delightful view

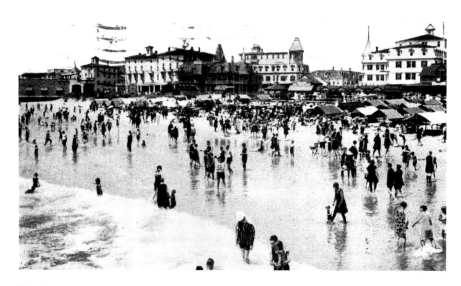

The famous Cape May strand proved to be the savior of the troubled resort after the 1878 fire. None of Cape May's competitors could offer the public the gentle sloping floor of beautiful white sand that had made Cape May famous. *Cape May County Historical Society; H. Gerald MacDonald.*

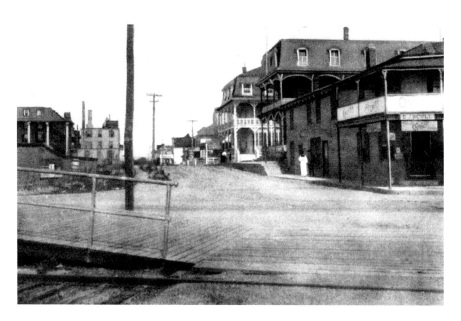

The city was rebuilt as a smaller, scaled-down version of itself after the 1878 fire. This decision preserved the intimate scale of the resort that is so valued today. Turn-of-the-century view of Perry Street taken from the boardwalk. *Author's collection.*

The Summer City by the Sea

of bathers during the bathing hours." This directory also described the impact that tourism had on the city's population: "The season for bathing commences about the 20th of June, and closes the 1st of September. A very small number of visitors is found there at either of those times; but, in the course of the season, it is estimated that as many as seventy-five thousand persons visit the place; and, during a portion of the time, there are as many as ten thousand at once, or, including children and servants, twelve thousand."

During the summer season, even government offices modified their schedules to suit vacationers. The directory noted that the post office's "summer arrangement" was "open for general business from 7 a.m. to 8:30 p.m., except Sundays and while sorting mail."

The beach became the engine that would drive the growth of the area destroyed by the fire. The "burned area" was too close to the Atlantic to remain undeveloped for long. The boardwalk was repaired to extend from Broadway to Madison Avenue. By 1880, Beach Drive and the Boardwalk were illuminated with gas lamps purchased by

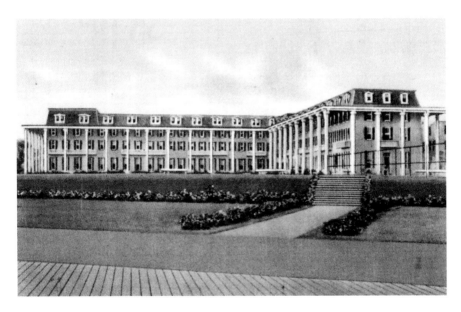

Congress Hall was rebuilt after the 1878 fire as a traditional L-shaped Cape May beachfront hotel. Brick was used in the construction of this smaller version of the grand old hotel in the hopes of fireproofing the building. *Author's collection.*

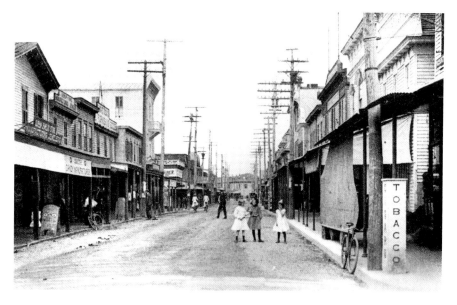

Washington Street, circa 1900, taken from Perry Street looking east. The commercial district survived the 1878 fire and remained unchanged for most of the twentieth century. *Author's collection.*

the city from the Pennsylvania Globe Gas Light Company. The lights were placed at equal distances, seventy paces, along the entire length of the boardwalk.

The *Cape May Wave* reported that "the effect thus produced being exceedingly brilliant and attractive," and all agreed that the city should be congratulated for this attempt to "beautify and improve this, the grandest of nature's gifts to us as a watering-place."

As competition with Atlantic City intensified, the *Cape May Wave* reported that while more than seventy Atlantic City hotels and boardinghouses advertised in local Atlantic City newspapers, clearly understanding the value of printer's ink, Cape May's lack of advertising caused the publisher to wonder if his paper was a breeder of "some dire pestilence."

Growth After the Fire

As the city was busy rebuilding, only the most optimistic citizens thought that Cape May had a chance of halting Atlantic City's rapid growth.

The new Congress Hall added a two-thousand-square-foot music pavilion designed by Stephen D. Button to its lawn. The United States Hotel (the old Sherman House) had survived the fire, and its proprietor, C.B. Reeves, was preparing it for the beginning of the new season. The Atlantic Hotel had perished in the fire, with insurance coverage totaling $18,000. The owner, E.C. Knight of Philadelphia, who had purchased the hotel for $24,000 just before the fire, decided not to rebuild it. (The site remained vacant for thirteen years after the 1878 fire until the Atlantic Terrace cottages were erected in 1891.)

The Brunswick House borrowed the name and became the new Atlantic. The Avenue House was rebuilt on the site of its namesake that was lost in the fire. Victor Denizot had the Ocean View cottage constructed at the foot of Decatur Street and replaced his wooden pier that had been lost in the fire.

The Windsor Hotel was opened for business in 1879 by its owner, Thomas Whitney. He had commissioned architect Button to add two wings to his existing cottage, located on the west side of Congress Street, and as previously noted, Button created a typical L-shaped Cape May beachfront hotel, reminiscent of the previous generation of hotels. The

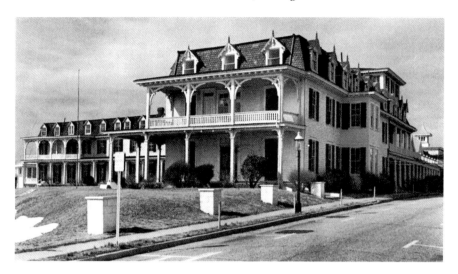

The Windsor Hotel was constructed in 1879 for Thomas Whitney with the addition of two large wings to his existing cottage located on Windsor Street and Beach Drive. Architect Stephen Decatur Button saw to it that the hotel took on the classic Cape May look when he was commissioned to design the addition (seen here). *Author's collection.*

Windsor was an example of the Second Empire style popular from 1850 to 1890.

One of the few hotels constructed after the fire in a contemporary style was the New Columbia, located on Jackson Street on the site of the old Merchant Hotel. The owner, James Mooney of Philadelphia, hired a Philadelphia architect and gave him free rein. The result was a 160-room hotel designed in the Queen Anne style popular between 1880 and 1900. The New Columbia, with its numerous towers and variety of textures, materials and colors, was a startling contrast to the traditional Cape May hotel.

The hotel was operated from 1879 to 1881 by Michael Ward, who leased it from Mooney for $6,000 per year. The large sum attests to the hotel's popularity, although during its short life (it burned to the ground in 1889), its architectural style was not adopted by any large-scale developer in the city.

Another addition to Jackson Street was the Carroll Villa, built for George Hildreth on the site of his Wyoming cottage that was lost in the fire. The builder followed the conservative taste of the city and designed the building in the American Bracketed Villa style, a hybrid of the

The Summer City by the Sea

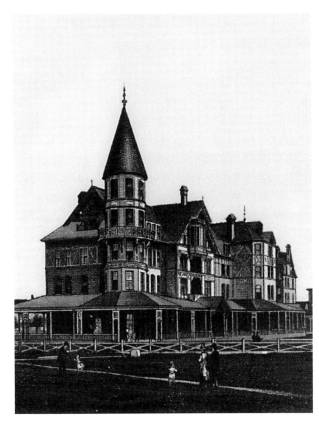

The New Columbia Hotel located on Jackson Street was constructed immediately after the fire of 1878. The designer of the hotel broke with Cape May tradition and constructed the building in the Queen Anne style. *Helenclare Leary.*

conservative Italianate style so loved by Stephen D. Button. The Carroll Villa still stands today at 19 Jackson Street.

Button was once more given the opportunity to leave his imprint on the Cape May landscape in 1881 when, at age sixty-eight, he was given the commission to design a beachfront hotel for Ocean Villa owner Victor Denizot.

The *Cape May Wave* reported on October 8, 1881, that "Mr. S.D Button, the well-known architect, has finished the plans for the proposed hotel of Councilman Denizot on Beach [Avenue]. Its sleeping apartments will number one hundred and twenty-five." Named the Lafayette Hotel, the design of the four-story building followed the standard L-shaped format, with Button incorporating an oversized veranda similar to the one he utilized in his Stockton House design twelve years earlier. The Lafayette opened for business in 1884. In 1883, the charming Star Villa, located on Ocean Street behind the Lafayette site, was constructed by different architects but in the Button style.

Of the four major hotels along Cape May's beachfront, three had been designed by Stephen D. Button (the Lafayette, Windsor and Stockton), and the new Congress Hall had hired him to supervise improvements shortly after it was built. Cape May approached the twentieth century with its major hotels and many of its cottages designed or influenced by a man born almost fifty years before the start of the Civil War.

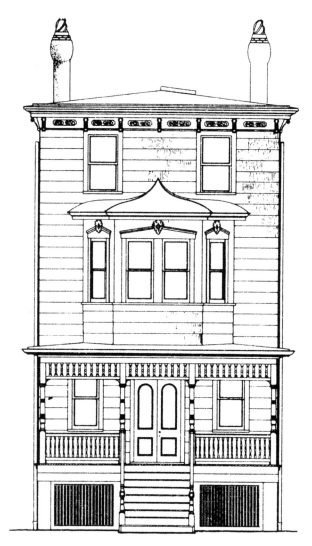

The Atlantic Terrace houses were designed by Stephen Decatur Button and constructed for E.C. Knight on the site of McMakin's Atlantic Hotel thirteen years after the old hotel was lost in the 1878 blaze. *Historical American Buildings Survey.*

On a spring day in 1884, an unusual structure began to take shape on the deserted beachfront meadows that separated the city of Cape May and Cape May Point. Crowds of children and adults gathered daily to witness the construction of a large wooden elephant. Named the "Light of Asia," the elephant was designed by Philadelphia architect N.H. Culver and was built for land speculator and entrepreneur Theodore M. Reger. (Culver was no doubt influenced by James V. Lafferty, designer of Lucy, the original Margate elephant, in 1881 and Elephantine Colossus, built at Coney Island, in 1882.)

Reger placed a display advertisement in local newspapers in June 1884 soliciting tenants for his colossal pachyderm. "Parties wishing rooms in the elephant to sell soda water, fancy articles, advertising, etc, and privilege for bathhouses, ice cream garden and dairy. Apply on the premises or to T.M. Reger, 508 Walnut Street, Philadelphia."

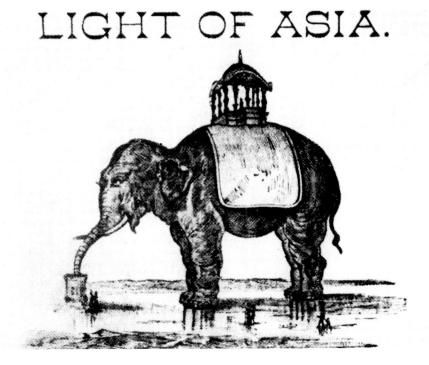

Theodore M. Reger advertised his "Light of Asia" in 1884 as an amusement attraction that would contain bathhouses and concessions. The observatory on the giant's back offered a view of the Atlantic Ocean. *Author's collection.*

Plans for the "Light of Asia" called for the wooden elephant to stand forty feet, ten inches tall. A "howdah," or covered pavilion, rested on the giant's back. The hind legs were equipped with spiral stairs that provided access to the interior of the elephant. Two sets of stairs on either side of the interior led to the howdah, where an observatory offered to tourists a scenic view of the Atlantic Ocean and surrounding meadows for ten cents. It was estimated that more than 1 million pieces of wood were required to construct the elephant, which was covered with a "skin" consisting of more than thirteen thousand square feet of tin.

The "Light of Asia" was eventually used by Reger and his associates to attract prospective land buyers to their new enterprise. Reger, along with Thomas H. Williamson and Albert B. Little, had incorporated the Neptune Land Company in 1882. Their goal was to develop the land where the old Mount Vernon had once stood. Known as the Mount Vernon tract, the site extended from the Sea Breeze excursion house on Grant Street west along the beachfront to the Weatherby tract that bordered the community of Cape May Point.

Although the great wooden creature attracted many sightseers, the tract developed at an elephant's pace. Before the Civil War, Philadelphian Mark Devine had begun purchasing land on Cape Island. He acquired the Mount Vernon tract in a series of purchases dating as far back as 1839. His holdings at the time of his death in 1885 stretched from present Patterson Avenue in the city of Cape May west to the Weatherby tract and north from the ocean to present-day Sunset Boulevard. Reger and his associates acquired part of the Devine property and reorganized as the Mount Vernon Land Company in 1887. A sign was painted across the wooden elephant's massive body, "New Mount Vernon."

Cape May resident F. Sidney Townsend wrote in his journal on March 3, 1889, "[T]here does not seem to be any prospect of business so far for the spring time except a small amount of work at the Mt. Vernon Land Co's land between this city and Cape May Point." He later noted on May 12 of the same year that "excursion came down from Philadelphia of about 150 Germans, some of them interested in the Mt. Vernon Land Co's lots."

A new small wooden hotel was constructed and named the Mount Vernon Hotel in honor of the massive structure that burned down in

The Summer City by the Sea

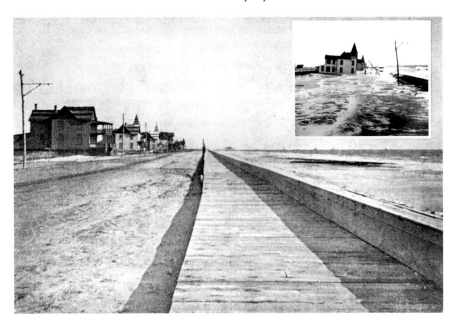

Beach Avenue from Twenty-first Street looking east. South Cape May was chartered as a borough in 1894, with oceanfront lots located between Seventh and Twenty-first Avenues. *Inset*: The sea eventually claimed the small borough as each successive storm took another bite out of the community. Many of the homes were moved to Cape May. *Richardson Collection/Cape May County Historical Society.*

1856. Lots were sold, and the area became known as Mount Vernon. The *Star of the Cape* ran a notice in 1889 reading, "The Mount Vernon Hotel and Lot Association, owners of the Mount Vernon Tract, Cape May, N.J., between 7th and 21st Avenue on the ocean front, lots for sale at very reasonable prices."

The tract developed slowly into a small community of beachfront cottages. Mount Vernon was chartered as the borough of South Cape May in 1894. Never a major success, the community's distance from the city of Cape May's urban center proved troublesome. Erosion and savage storms raged a continuous battle for possession of the community until the weatherworn borough of South Cape May was finally dissolved in 1945. Many of the South Cape May homes were moved to the eastern section of the Devine tract, as far east as Broadway.

The Mount Vernon Land Company was not the only enterprise to attempt to develop the Devine tract. The Cape May City Land

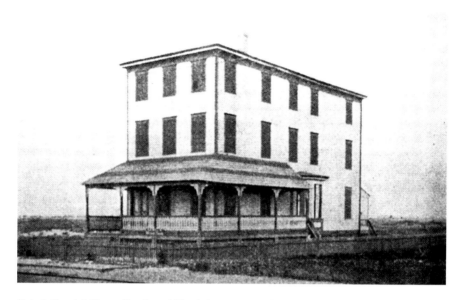

Gabels Beach Villa, at Beach and Tenth Avenues, was featured in a Mount Vernon Land Company promotional brochure. The site has since been claimed by the Atlantic. *Richardson Collection/Cape May County Historical Society.*

Company was organized, and it subdivided lots on the eastern section of the tract from Patterson Avenue west to Seventh Avenue in 1882. The tract extended north from the ocean to Cape Island Creek. Fifth Avenue connected north with the Steamboat Landing Turnpike—or Sunset Boulevard, as it is called today. Though some lots were sold because of the tract's proximity to the city, the venture eventually collapsed.

By 1899, 140 lots in the area from Patterson Avenue west to Second Avenue were still being advertised for sale by the executor of Elizabeth Devine's estate. These are the only streets that still exist today; the streets west of Second Avenue have been claimed over the years by erosion. Another venture, the Cape May Beach Land Company, attempted to develop the Weatherby tract, between Cape May Point and South Cape May, sometime after 1908, but the enterprise was not successful.

THE *REPUBLIC* ERA

On June 17, 1888, F. Sidney Townsend noted in his journal that "the *Republic* brought an excursion today of about 1600." The last and grandest descendant of the long line of luxury side-wheel steamers that carried vacationers between Philadelphia and Cape May City, the *Republic* operated from 1878 to 1903. (Its name was changed to the *Cape May* during its last year of operation, 1903.)

Travelers bound for Cape May would board the beautiful, three-deck iron vessel at the wharf at the foot of Race Street, Philadelphia, and for one dollar (fifty cents each way), they could relax on the *Republic*'s promenade as the vessel meandered down the Delaware River. The steamboat, which was advertised in the city's 1881 directory as the "Mammoth Palace Steamer," could carry up to three thousand passengers.

The *Republic* offered a dining saloon where breakfast, dinner and supper were served. The steamboat provided a civil means of travel that many still preferred to the railroads. Bands would serenade the passengers as they traveled along at fifteen knots, enjoying the same view from the river that their grandparents had sixty years earlier.

The *Republic* would dock at the steamboat wharf on the Delaware Bay side of Cape May Point. The Delaware Bay House, located at the landing, was a fully equipped excursion house that provided for the needs of the vacationers as they disembarked from the steamer.

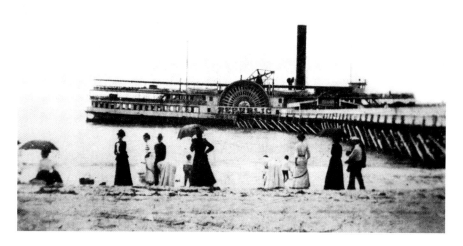

Summer "loiterers" await the arrival of the luxury steamer *Republic*. The popular steamboat operated from 1878 to 1903 and provided round-trip transportation between Philadelphia and Cape May for one dollar. *Cape May County Historical Society.*

The owner of the *Republic*, Jonathan Cone, seeking a more efficient mode of transporting his customers from the landing to the city, organized the Delaware Bay and Cape May Railroad to run along the beach from the steamboat landing to Cape May City. Although he indirectly competed with the railroads for the Cape May tourist trade, Cone enjoyed a cozy relationship with the West Jersey Railroad and its directors. Railroad management realized that by transporting steamboat travelers on his short line along the beach to West Jersey's Grant Street station, Cone was contributing to their business, as many chose to take the train back to Philadelphia. Contemporary maps indicate that tracks ran parallel to Sunset Boulevard providing steamboat travelers with a second rail line to the city center or the Grant Street station.

The schedule for the Delaware Bay and Cape May Railroad, appearing in the June 17, 1882 *Cape May Wave*, advertised daily trains to Cape May City starting at 6:30 a.m. The trip took about ten minutes. Except for the "steamboat train," which was an express to the city, the train occasionally made a flag stop at Cape May Point.

The Summer City by the Sea

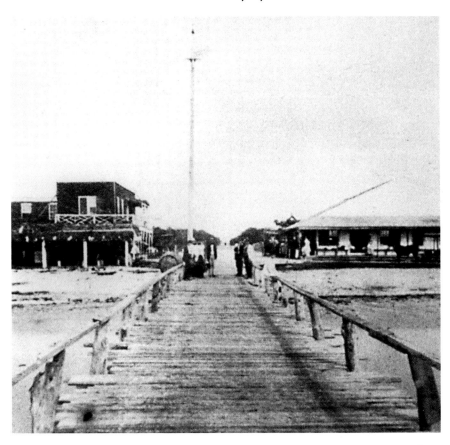

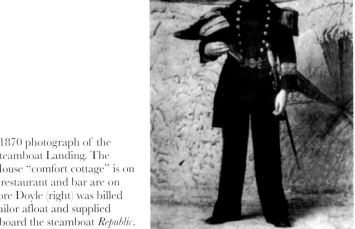

This page: Circa 1870 photograph of the Delaware Bay Steamboat Landing. The Delaware Bay House "comfort cottage" is on the left, and the restaurant and bar are on right. Commodore Doyle (right) was billed as the smallest sailor afloat and supplied entertainment aboard the steamboat *Republic*. *Cape May County Historical Society.*

Specially designated trains connected with lines on the West Jersey Railroad. The newspaper ad also noted that the short line connected with trains on the Cape May and Sewell's Point Railroad. This line consisted of a horse trolley that traveled from the excursion house along the beach east to Madison Avenue, where a steam locomotive completed the trip to Sewell's Point and the popular Inlet House.

The Delaware Bay and Cape May Railroad began to feel competition from the Delaware Bay and Sewell's Point Railroad, an electric trolley line that traveled from the Grant Street station vicinity along the beach to the pavilion at Cape May Point. The new line's tracks paralleled the older company's rails along most of the beach. In 1893, the two railroads merged and formed the Cape May, Delaware Bay and Sewell's Point Railroad. The combined company's parallel tracks now formed a double-track line to Cape May Point.

The West Jersey Railroad merged with the Camden and Atlantic in 1896 and became the West Jersey and Seashore Railroad, which was controlled by the Pennsylvania Railroad. The West Jersey and Seashore line compensated the Cape May, Delaware Bay and Sewell's Point Railroad to provide winter service, connecting its Grant Street summer station with its winter station located on Jackson Street. During the off-season, the smaller railroad would run its trains on the West Jersey's tracks, 0.65 mile to the winter station.

Records indicate that this agreement became strained when the Cape May, Delaware Bay and Sewell's Point line decided to switch to its parallel electric trolley tracks, which deposited passengers in front of the Grant Street station instead of inside it. A compromise was reached allowing for the passengers' baggage to be transported from the trolley to the inside of the Grant Street terminal. This arrangement between the two lines continued into the early part of the twentieth century.

Cape May approached the twentieth century desperately seeking that elusive "improvement" needed to catapult it back to its former status as Queen of the Seaside Resorts. Observing the success that the "iron pier" was reaping for its competitors, Cape May constructed one of its own. The July 19, 1884 *Wave* observed, "It is becoming daily more settled in the minds of our visitors and residents that the pier will not only be the center of Cape May's life and attractions, but that it will pay handsomely as an investment."

The Summer City by the Sea

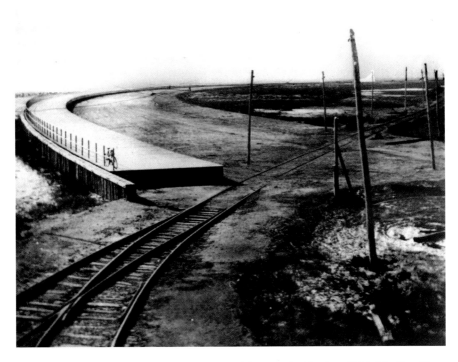

Sewell's Point, the abrupt terminus of the Cape May boardwalk, circa 1906. The Sewell's Point Railroad combined horse trolleys and steam locomotives to transport tourists from Cape May Point to the popular Inlet House on Sewell's Point. *H. Gerald MacDonald.*

Built by the Phoenix Iron Company, the partially completed pier was opened for the 1884 season. The iron structure extended one thousand feet over the Atlantic Ocean. Complete with an outdoor pavilion, the pride of the resort contained over half an acre of floor space with an eight-thousand-square-foot dance floor. The outdoor pavilion was eventually enclosed for use for band concerts, hops, theater and light opera. The second or lower level of the pier provided facilities for sport fishing, and the outer end of the structure was used as a wharf.

Another improvement was noted by Cape May resident F. Sidney Townsend in his journal on July 27, 1888. "Great preparations are being made for the opening of the Driving Park Association tomorrow. It is expected to have four running races and 3000 people." He was referring to the Cape May Driving Park, an oval horse track organized by James Edmunds in West Cape May. Edmunds had been one of Theodore

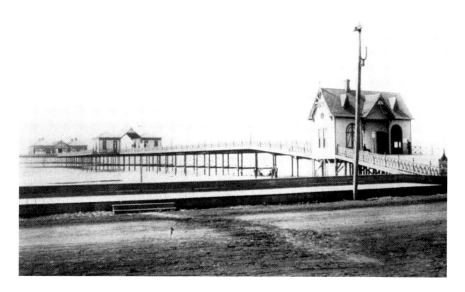

The Cape May iron pier, constructed in 1884, was the most popular attraction in the resort in the late nineteenth century. Extending one thousand feet over the ocean, the pier provided an outdoor pavilion for dancing and a lower deck for fishing. *Cape May County Historical Society.*

Reger's partners in the Mount Vernon Land Company enterprise in South Cape May.

The opening-day races were witnessed by more than three thousand people, and the venture looked like a sure thing. Unfortunately the novelty quickly wore off, and a hoped-for railroad spur that would connect the park to the city never materialized. Without this lifeline to the resort, the park was doomed. Adding to the park's problems was Cape May's increasingly conservative politics and its intolerance of gambling, amusements and alcohol consumption. Many full-time residents were happy to see the park fail.

Year-round residents of Cape May attempted to instill their conservative philosophies on the summer visitors and went so far as to vote the city "dry" in a local election, delivering a massive blow to the city's hotels and chasing away visitors in droves. An 1897 state constitutional amendment banning gambling ended another popular seaside pastime.

Tensions began to mount between the conservative permanent residents, who had the right to vote, and the cottagers, who were growing weary of taxation without representation. A group of cottagers, several with significant investments in the resort, organized the Cape May Cottagers Association in 1891 to protect their interests.

Many were concerned over the fact that the old resort, unable to attract enough capital to compete with Atlantic City and its high-tech amusements, was beginning to market itself as a wholesome alternative. The *Cape May Wave* editorialized, "The amusement of the average watering resort today is a disease, and one of those chronic affections which is infectious to every person and thing which comes in contact, the American public has conceded the fact that Cape May is virtuous."

The public may have admired Cape May's virtue, but as far as their vacations were concerned, the growing middle class headed to Long Branch and Atlantic City by the hundreds of thousands. The society set continued to abandon Cape May for fashionable Newport, and as the old watering place grew more and more conservative, outside investors looked elsewhere.

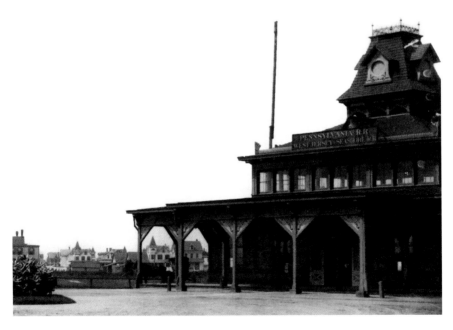

The West Jersey and Seashore Railroad was the result of the merger of the West Jersey Railroad and the Camden and Atlantic in 1896. The new railroad was controlled by the Pennsylvania Railroad. The "summer station," located on Grant Street, was operated only during the summer tourist season. *H. Gerald MacDonald.*

Permanent residents did approve of athletics, and the Cape May Athletic Club was organized. Attractions such as baseball, bicycling, racing, boxing and wrestling entertained the summer visitors. It became a common practice for vacationing college players to play for the Cape May Athletic Club team against visiting semiprofessional teams.

As the 1899 season drew to a close, fire again struck the city. It came on the heels of several years of, as a resident noted, "dull seasons." The fire began at about 1:00 a.m. on September 25, 1889. This time, the victim was the unique New Columbia, built only ten years earlier. The New Columbia's use of brick in its construction was thought to offer a degree of fire resistance to the structure, but that did not prove to be the case on that rainy night. The fire quickly engulfed the hotel and spread with such velocity that the proprietor, F.H. Hildreth, and his wife barely escaped.

The city fire department successfully contained the flames, and adjacent buildings experienced only minor damage. Townsend noted the possible cause of the blaze in his journal on September 29, 1889: "The theory of the burning of the hotel is that it was fired by the explosion of a gas meter…even the bricks are so broken that a large majority of them are worthless…I never saw anything so completely a total loss as that structure…a wooden building could not have been more thoroughly consumed."

To add to the resort's problems, legions of hungry mosquitoes descended on the city and made life unbearable. A resident wrote in 1888 of "swarms of mosquitoes…never saw the likes of for fifteen years." Many tourists cut their vacations short due to the voracious pest. They were everywhere. "Even bedrooms are full of them," noted Townsend in his diary.

On an optimistic note, Townsend wrote the following year that "the papers say that a new railroad company has obtained a charter ostensibly to run to Cape May between Winslow Junction and Sea Isle City, in the end it will reach Cape May City which is hoped it will before the beginning of another season."

The new railroad was enthusiastically anticipated as a means of expansion for the city. Because the terminus of the railroad in the city was to be at Ocean and Washington Streets, several stores and small boardinghouses, including the Delaware House, were removed to

The Summer City by the Sea

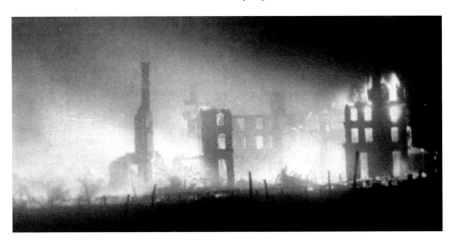

Although the New Columbia Hotel was thought to be fireproof, it burned to the ground in 1889. The new and improved city fire department contained the fire and prevented another citywide conflagration. *Cape May County Historical Society.*

accommodate the station. The railroad began its life as the Tuckahoe and Cape May Railroad in 1890. It was later sold at foreclosure in March 1894 to the Cape May Railroad, which completed the connection to Cape May City before merging with the South Jersey Railroad in 1894. Both companies eventually became part of the Atlantic City Railroad, which was owned by the Reading Railroad.

The existing West Jersey Railroad, part of the Pennsylvania Railroad, did not want to lose its transportation monopoly to the resort and obtained a court injunction to prevent the new railroad from crossing its tracks one mile south of Woodbine, New Jersey. The court eventually ruled that the Cape May Railroad could not cross the existing tracks at grade but had to construct an overhead bridge. It was forbidden from placing a diamond at the crossing.

To ensure that the court's will was enforced, the West Jersey positioned an engine on its tracks complete with a watchman where the upstart railroad's diamond would have to be positioned. The Cape May Railroad would not be denied, and one evening it sent the diamond on a flatcar along with a small army of club-wielding men. As the crew began to unload the diamond, a West Jersey train arrived with a small army of its own. A battle ensued, and as the Italian and Irish rail crews clashed, a couple of the Cape May Railroad's workers managed to install the diamond. The first train entered Cape May on June 23, 1894. The South Jersey, as it was renamed, eventually constructed the court-ordered overhead bridge and the diamond was removed.

The entire city declared a holiday as trainloads of railroad officials and vacationers arrived. The South Jersey carried more than two thousand excursionists at no charge to inspect the city. A number of hotels—the Lafayette, Congress Hall, Windsor, Chalfonte and Marine Villa—agreed to entertain the visitors at their own expense. The city was decorated complete with a massive evergreen welcoming arch at the new station. Several hotel bands provided music as the first train pulled into town.

Newspapers announced, "Through the perseverance and managerial ability of Cape May's champions, the Queen of Resorts is more closely linked to the large cities." A bold headline exclaimed, "The New Era…The Renaissance," and heralded the organizers as heroes of the day, proclaiming, "Cape May had been Rescued." The editor went on to say that "the affairs have so shaped themselves during the last two years of the resort's history to be termed critical. There has been so to speak, a hanging in the balance, a turning point…which meant in one direction…a degeneracy, or fall into insignificance, in the other direction was prosperity."

In the pre-automobile era, a city was dependent on the railroads for its link with the world and its survival. A city like Cape May, located on the isolated Jersey peninsula, was even more dependent on the iron road. The tone of the newspaper article attests to the desperate state of the city as the clock ran down on the nineteenth century.

Unfortunately, the timing for a renaissance could not have been worse. The resort and the entire country were in the grip of a terrible depression triggered by the financial panic of 1893. By December 1893, more than six hundred banks had failed nationwide, and by June of the following year, more than 190 railroads had gone bust. In an effort to consolidate costs, the South Jersey's Cape May competitor, the West Jersey and Atlantic Railroad, along with five other lines, became part of the newly organized West Jersey and Seashore Railroad Company on May 4, 1896. By the winter of 1893–94, more than 2.5 million people were out of work, and few Americans could afford a seaside vacation.

However, two more hotels were constructed in the city at the end of the nineteenth century. The first, the Baltimore Inn, located on Jackson

The Summer City by the Sea

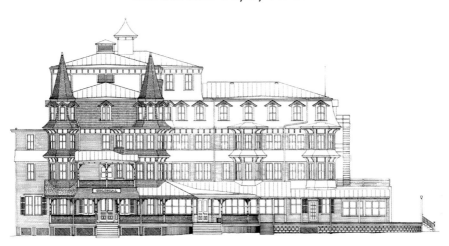

The Colonial Hotel was built in 1894–95 and still stands on Beach Avenue and Ocean Street. The hotel was successful enough to warrant the addition of a new wing in 1905. *Historical American Buildings Survey.*

Street, was built during 1892 and 1893, and the second, the Colonial, on Ocean Street above Beach Drive, was constructed during 1894 and 1895. The south wing of the Colonial was added in 1905. The depression and capital shortage probably explain the smaller size of the buildings compared to traditional Cape May hotels.

NEW JERSEY NEWPORT

The depression brought to a halt any expansion in Cape May. The newspapers listed hundreds of properties available at sheriff's sale. It would take the discovery of gold in the Klondike in the Yukon territory on August 12, 1896, to trigger the nation's second great gold rush (1897–98) and to lead the way to economic recovery. The *Star of the Cape* promised its readers that the Alaska gold discovery and the passage of the tariff bill would assist in setting the wheels of business into "active motion."

The Cape May Board of Trade was incorporated in 1897 as a vehicle to guide the resort into the next, and hopefully prosperous, century. This group of businessmen had its work cut out for it. Cape May was entering the new century threatened by more successful and modern competitors with new buildings constructed of brick and iron. Cape May's older hotels were out of fashion, and even its newer ones had the appearance of belonging to the dying century.

Smarting from the loss of business and in an obvious reference to Atlantic City, the *Star of the Cape* editor Aaron W. Hand wrote in 1897, "There are many people who think that the pathway to success in business is to be found in the crushing out by malediction and insane persecution of all business rivals. But unfortunately the rivals stay right on. The public is not as blind, deaf and dumb as such men imagine." As its first act, the board of trade appointed a committee to place advertisements in the Philadelphia newspapers in an effort to attract vacationers to Cape May.

As the century came to a close, the citizens of Cape May hoped and prayed for a new great era. The newspapers reported that never before in the city's history had so many people been on the streets at the midnight hour as there were at the close of the nineteenth century: "As the large gong in the town clock upon the top of the Methodist Church struck the hour of twelve a conglomeration of noises, which surely must have been heard by 'Uncle Eph' upon his shoally domain several miles out into the Atlantic, began." Whistles shrieked, bells in all the church steeples rang, guns were fired, tin horns tooted, firecrackers exploded and "a general racket ensued."

The new century appeared to get off to a hopeful start with promising news of the Queen Anne Connection. An ancestor of the Cape May/Lewes Ferry, the connection consisted of a steamer, *New Brunswick*, that began regular service between Cape May and Lewes, Delaware, in the summer of 1900, providing a link with Baltimore via the Queen Anne Railroad. The steamer anchored at the new iron pier in Cape May. The papers noted they hoped that "the Queen Anne Connection would open a new doorway for travel from Southern cities" and reassured all that "there is no reason why the people of the South should not make this their favorite resort."

The principal hotels preparing for the new century were Congress Hall, the Brexton, Marine Villa, Chalfonte, Windsor, Colonial, Stockton, Lafayette and the Ebbitt (later renamed the Virginia Hotel).

The resort's prayers seemed to be answered when a group of businessmen from Philadelphia and Pittsburgh planned a venture that they believed would transform the undeveloped eastern section of the city into a resort that would rival Newport.

While the papers began mentioning this project as early as 1901, work did not begin until the Cape May Real Estate Company was incorporated in March 1903. Originally known as the East Cape May Improvement Company, the reorganized Cape May Real Estate Company consisted of a new breed of developers. Although there were the usual Philadelphians involved, there was also William Flinn of Pittsburgh—whom the *New York Times* had just listed as the wealthiest of the new breed of Pittsburgh's coal, steel and oil millionaires—and Frank Edwards of Bristol, Pennsylvania. This was a major change for Cape May; most of the previous development in the city had originated from the Quaker City. So taken was the city with the infusion of new blood and capital that the locals began referring to the group as the "Pittsburgh Syndicate."

The promoters' vision of a modern city with connections to the major railroads and a new harbor that would rival the ports of Philadelphia and New York City excited the citizens of the depressed resort and promised to restore the city as a major seaside player.

The incorporation papers reported a capital stock of $750,000, and offices were promptly established in Cape May, Philadelphia and Pittsburgh. The new corporation promised a great deal and attempted to coerce the town into underwriting the improvements that would be needed to begin the development of the area east of Madison Avenue.

A group of citizens who had witnessed land schemes over the years protested the city absorbing all of the improvement costs. A letter to the editor of the *Star of the Cape* reminded readers that "the first duty of electors in a little place like Cape May is to resist such demands of private corporations as would lead to a surrender of municipal franchises" and therefore higher taxes. A costly but necessary improvement was the extension of both the existing boardwalk and Beach Drive eastward to the new development, along with a seawall to protect them. A compromise was reached: the Cape May Real Estate Company agreed to pay one-third of the cost of the extension and seawall, not to exceed $50,000. It also agreed to assume half of the cost of the essential sewer improvements.

The jewels in the crown of the new development were to be a million-dollar hotel and a harbor with a water area of five hundred acres and a depth of forty feet that the developers promised would be sufficient to float the largest ocean steamships ever built. Newspapers reported that the city of Philadelphia viewed the new harbor as a "formidable rival for its commerce."

A full-color broadside produced by the company promised that the new development would be an extraordinary investment opportunity, as well as a new and great future for "this famous resort." It warned potential investors not to miss this opportunity: "The remarkable history

The Summer City by the Sea

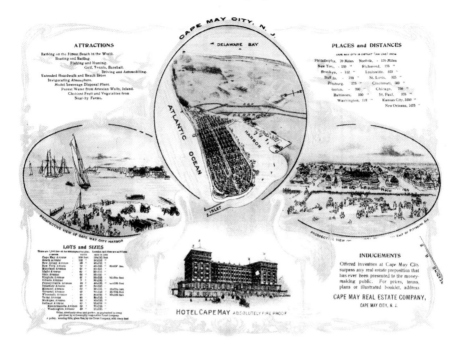

The Cape May Real Estate Company published a full-color broadside promising to "surpass any real estate proposition that has ever been presented to the money-making public." Featured prominently in the promotional brochure were the new Cape May City Harbor and the fireproof Hotel Cape May. *Helenclare Leary.*

of real estate in Atlantic City, where immense fortunes have been realized within ten years, where a small outlay a single decade ago has at the present day grown into millions, is bound to repeat itself in Cape May."

The syndicate described the five monster dredges that were engaged in creating the new harbor and filling the new land; 7,500 building lots were laid out on streets named after states and major cities.

The older section of Cape May, in anticipation, began to prepare itself for the growth that the new venture would bring to the city. The Sea Breeze Hotel was razed, and the newspapers reported that "after half a century, existence must give way to improvement" and promised that a modern hotel would soon take its place. A reporter predicted that "it is apparent that this is only the beginning of the many improvements that will follow in the near future and so transform this popular old seaside resort that many lifelong visitors will find it almost impossible to recognize the place."

Seven months later, the site of the demolished Sea Breeze excursion house was used as a storage site for the pilings needed for the new East Cape May bulkhead; the new hotel never materialized.

The promoters of the new tract scheduled an excursion to witness the starting of the monstrous dredging machine by the new Cape May Beach Syndicate. Regular daily rail excursions to the city had been discontinued for several years. Hundreds of visitors from a half-dozen states watched the dredge Pittsburgh at Schellinger's Landing. (Pittsburgh was actually the second dredge used on the project; the first was the J.B. Sandford, which began work on July 7, 1903.)

The Pennsylvania and the Philadelphia and Reading Railroads provided two special trains to transport prospective land buyers to the ceremony. The VIPs were met at the station by a reception committee and taken aboard trolley cars to Madison Avenue to view the new sewage disposal plant under construction. From there they proceeded to the dredge, where the work of forming the five-hundred-acre harbor had already commenced. At an appointed time, the ceremony of christening and naming the Pittsburgh took place.

The city suspended all business between 11:30 a.m. and 3:00 p.m. so all of the residents could witness the demonstration. The VIPs were then escorted to Congress Hall for a light supper, and by 3:45 p.m., special

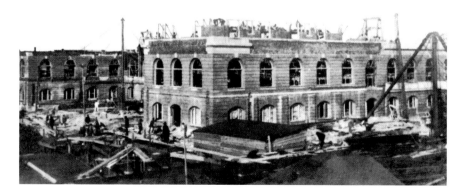

The Hotel Cape May was the "jewel in the crown" of the Cape May Real Estate Company syndicate. A 1906 photograph captured the partially completed hotel that took more than four years to complete. *H. Gerald MacDonald.*

trains began returning the guests to Philadelphia. Before departing, the visitors were encouraged to peruse the watercolor drawings of the harbor and the plans for the new hotel to be called, in case they didn't get the message, the New Cape May (later changed to Hotel Cape May).

By September 1904, the Cape May Real Estate Company was continuing to develop its "3600-acre property which extended along the beach for nearly two and one-half miles and inland for a mile... the material pumped from the harbor was used to fill portions of the adjacent tract."

The filling was up to grade from the beach to Washington Street, and the new ninety-foot-wide New Jersey Avenue was about to be opened and graveled to facilitate moving the trolley tracks from the beach to the new street. The Philadelphia and Reading Railroad had agreed to remove the trolley tracks three hundred feet inland from Beach Drive.

The sewage disposal plant on Madison Avenue near Washington Street was made ready for the installation of the electric pumps, which would

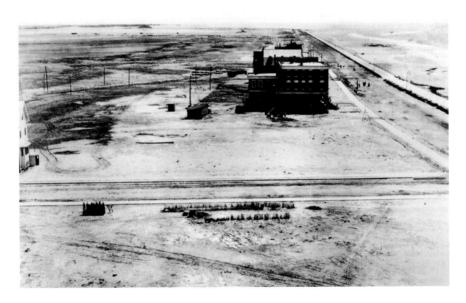

A 1906 photograph taken from the partially completed Hotel Cape May attests to the barren appearance of the undeveloped East Cape May tract. The boardwalk on the upper right of the image was completed to Sewell's Point to facilitate the new land scheme. *H. Gerald MacDonald.*

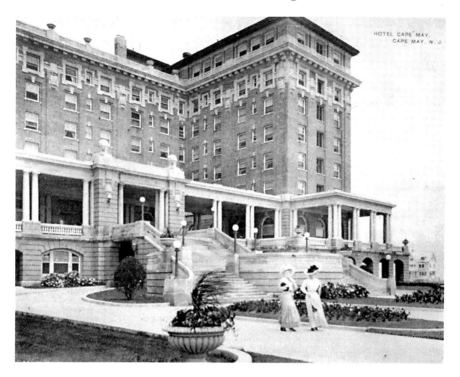

Early view of the Hotel Cape May, taken at the time of the 1908 grand opening. The celebration featured a visit from the governor of New Jersey and an automobile rally from Philadelphia to Cape May. *Cape May County Historical Society.*

transport all of the sewage from old and new Cape May nearly four miles across the county into Delaware Bay; the twenty-six-inch cast-iron sewer pipes had been laid during the previous summer.

Work on the Hotel Cape May began in 1905. The newly organized Cape May Automobile Club provided publicity for the project by sponsoring automobile races on the beach in front of the partially completed structure. Pioneer automobile promoters Henry Ford and Louis Chevrolet participated in the races along the strand between Madison Avenue and Sewell's Point. (Ford purchased property in the vicinity, which prompted rumors that he planned to establish an automobile plant in Cape May. A spokesman for Ford issued a statement that the company had no such plans.)

The million-dollar work in progress began to experience major problems that the syndicate unsuccessfully attempted to conceal from the public. Various construction mishaps and labor disputes, along with the constant pilfering of building material, delayed the projected opening of the hotel by two years. When it was finally completed in 1908, the cost had more than doubled, and the Cape May Real Estate Company was on the verge of bankruptcy. All aspects of the overly ambitious project, including dredging and land reclamation, were much more costly than the original projections. The dredge Pittsburgh sank in November 1910 just offshore of Pittsburgh Avenue when a large rock was drawn into its suction pipe, destroying its twelve-foot pump and allowing water to fill the dredge. The eight-man crew barely escaped, just clearing the dredge before it went to the bottom.

Though lots were slowly selling, few cottages were erected. As late as July 1907, Dr. Walter Starr of Philadelphia was being hailed by the papers as the "pioneer cottage-builder in New Cape May" and was complimented on his attractive white cottage at the corner of New Jersey and Baltimore Avenues.

As the dredges worked day and night filling in the lowlands for the Newport of New Jersey, the Hotel Cape May finally opened in the spring of 1908.

Attending the opening celebration were state and local dignitaries, including the governor of New Jersey, George E. Fort, who presented the Hotel Cape May Cup to the happy winner of the road-ability contest, an automobile rally from Philadelphia to Cape May. More than forty cars left the Quaker City between noon and 1:30 p.m., and most arrived at the resort in time for the dinner reception.

The opening of the million-dollar Hotel Cape May was hailed by the local newspapers as one of the greatest events that had ever occurred in Cape May. Still optimistic, the press noted that considering the millions of dollars expended by the Cape May Real Estate Company, the United States government, the railroads and the city, "No sane person now has any doubt of Cape May becoming a great and popular seaside resort." An editorial promised that the hotel would "stand in all future time as the beginning of a Greater Cape May…which will make all past history of the resort pale and insignificant." This was not to be.

In October 1908, six months after it opened, the hotel was mysteriously closed for repairs. The *Cape May Star and Wave* reported the news and

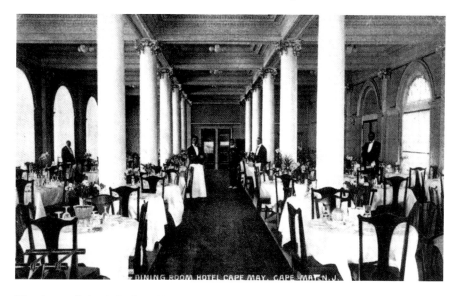

The elegant dining hall of the Hotel Cape May as it appeared during the grand opening celebration. The local press hailed the opening of the hotel as one of the greatest events in Cape May history. *Author's collection.*

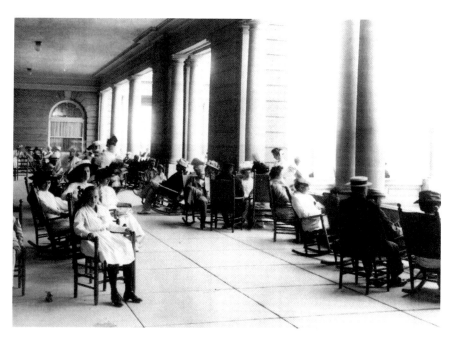

Ghosts of another era, passing a lazy summer afternoon "rocker style" on the porch of the Hotel Cape May, circa 1915. *Library of Congress.*

then warned its readers that "if there is anybody in Cape May disposed to hinder its [the Hotel Cape May] progress they are not friends of the resort," further assuring them that the venture had created invaluable assets for the city.

All of the rhetoric could not hide the bleak financial fact that the entire venture was about to collapse. Corporation president Peter Shields accepted the inevitable and resigned. The closing of the hotel marked the end of new construction and the termination of the harbor dredging. By 1910, the only mention of the enterprise in the local papers was a report concerning architect Frederick J. Osterling's suit against the Cape May Hotel Company for $45,000 in unpaid fees, which he eventually won.

Just as it appeared that all was lost, a savior arrived in the person of Nelson Zuinglius Graves, a Philadelphia manufacturer and longtime Cape May cottager. He became the project director in 1911 and was considered a local hero by the believers in the "New Jersey Newport." He immediately purchased the Cape May Light and Power Company from the failing syndicate and the trolley line from the Reading. The harbor was completed with the help of the dredge Nelson Z. Graves as its owner supervised the construction of the amusement casino—or "fun factory," as it was known—on Sewell's Point.

The city, in an effort to see the project to completion, made additional tax concessions to Graves. Several new cottages were constructed, including Graves's cottage on New Jersey Avenue and the William Sewell Jr. cottage on Beach Avenue.

The project progressed at a snail's pace until another economic slowdown broke the highly leveraged Graves. The Cape May Real Estate Company followed Graves to bankruptcy court, and the remaining lots of the "New Jersey Newport" were sold at auction to pay delinquent taxes. The eastern third of the New Cape May property was acquired by the United States Navy during World War I and was used to erect a base.

The ill-fated Hotel Cape May never fulfilled its promise to restore Cape May to the throne of Queen of the Seaside Resorts. Instead of becoming a magnet attracting investors to the city, the hotel remained empty after the collapse of the Cape May Real Estate Company. It was used as a military hospital during World War I and as a U.S. Naval Annex house during World War II.

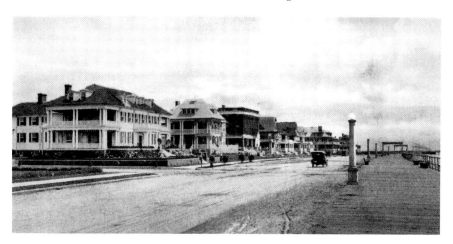

Early twentieth-century view of Beach Drive and the cottages that gradually filled the East Cape May Company tract after the failure of the "New Jersey Newport." Many cottagers acquired their lots at auctions held to pay the delinquent taxes of the developer. *Author's collection.*

The hotel was later acquired by the Admiral Hotel Company, which attempted to operate it as a hotel. The effort failed, and the city took the hotel over for back taxes in 1940. The building was then sold to a Philadelphia realty company that considered developing it into a senior citizens home. Fundamentalist preacher Carl McIntire purchased the hotel and saved it from the wrecker's ball in 1963.

This project, which was to transform Cape May into the Newport of New Jersey, was the last major expansion effort in the city until its renaissance half a century later. The harbor that was to become a rival of New York and Philadelphia is now predominantly used by pleasure craft. The Hotel Cape May, after operating unsuccessfully as the Admiral Hotel and later the Christian Admiral Hotel, fell to the wrecking ball in 1996.

Ironically, the failure of the venture to modernize the city by tearing down the old and constructing a new brick and steel copycat of its neighbor to the north unknowingly saved the quaint wooden seaside village for a renaissance later in the century.

Cool Cape May

The failure of the East Cape May project, combined with the city's numerous concessions to the real estate syndicate, demoralized and angered the citizenry of the beleaguered resort.

The newspapers that had originally enthusiastically supported the project now chastised the city's officials:

> *Cape May Alone In This....Neither Wildwood, Ocean City nor Atlantic City permits its city treasury to be used, directly or indirectly, to supply the funds for the carrying out of the schemes of the various real estate syndicates in it...Cape May is probably the only city in the wide world that is forced by one means or another to become a partner with every real estate syndicate which attempts to do business here, with the results that it has been nearly eaten up alive.*

The city that once owned the coveted transportation monopoly, the powerful river highway connection with Philadelphia, was now almost forgotten in the train and automobile era. Land transportation was king, and Cape May's location at the far tip of the Jersey peninsula, along with an inadequate road system, combined to turn the Queen of the Seaside Resorts into an isolated, provincial seaside village.

This is not to say that the city did not have a loyal group of cottagers and vacationers, but its base was dwindling each year. Tension simmered as the summer cottagers and full-time residents blamed each other for the city's demise. With few exceptions, Cape May would change little over the next fifty years.

The aging Stockton Hotel was torn down in 1910, supposedly to make way for new construction. The reality was that the city block where the once-magnificent hotel stood would remain empty until 1914. No large modern hotel was built on the site, and the block was subdivided into lots to accommodate cottages, the First Baptist Church (today Cape Island Baptist) and the smaller New Stockton Villa (constructed in 1914 at Beach Drive and Howard Street and now the Hotel Macomber).

The mosquitoes that had plagued the resort for decades and ruined many summer seasons were finally taken seriously in 1912. The state legislature approved the first county commission law that empowered Cape May County to establish the Cape May County Mosquito Commission. The local paper announced, "The Mosquito is Doomed."

Commission president L.C. Ogden met with fellow commissioners throughout the state to gather the latest information on eradicating the pest. The commission waged war on the hated insect by attacking its

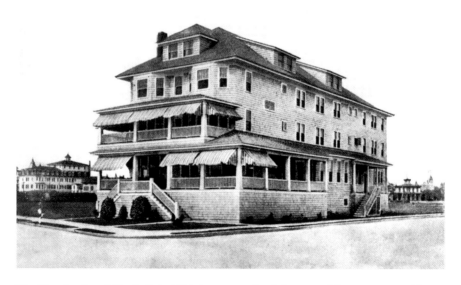

The New Stockton Villa, built in 1914, is an example of the turn-of-the-century trend in Cape May toward smaller, more manageable hotels. Known today as the Macomber, the structure still stands on Beach Drive and Howard Street. *Author's collection.*

breeding grounds and draining the lowlands. As anyone who attempts to spend time outdoors on a warm summer evening can attest, the tiny pest is still a formidable foe.

It would take the war in Europe to revive the city's economy. Visitors during the summer of 1915 witnessed the flotilla of naval ships anchored in the newly created Cape May Harbor. Rumors began to circulate that the navy planned to establish a base, complete with an aviation field, at Sewell's Point on property owned by the Cape May Real Estate Company.

The Bethlehem Steel Company established a munitions testing complex on the cape at present-day Higbee's Beach. The city welcomed the company and the additional business it would bring the city with a grand parade. Bethlehem Steel had contracts with the Russian, British and French governments to produce munitions. The shells were transported to Cape May by train, loaded onto trucks and taken to Higbee's Beach for testing. A narrow-gauge railway carried the shells over the dunes to the testing site.

Rumors of the navy base became fact when the government began to deepen the harbor channel to accommodate submarines.

In 1917, when President Woodrow Wilson asked Congress for a declaration of war against Germany, work began immediately on the new base and aviation field, Cape May Section Base No. 9. Navy personnel had chosen the empty "fun factory" on Sewell's Point for their new facility and had taken over the land from Yale Avenue to Sewell's Point. Retired Lieutenant Commandant USNR Frederick A. Savage described the facility in an article published in 1942: "There was an old amusement pavilion at Sewell's Point which had been out of use for two years. The windows were all broken, drifted sand was all over everything, the road was covered and almost four feet of sand had drifted in on the floor of the skating rink, but on our recommendation, this site was selected as the best available for the purpose." The skating rink was converted into a mess hall and sleeping quarters, with the old stage filling in as a galley. The base's primary function was to provide operational support to the submarine chasers and minesweepers in the area.

Patriotism, along with anticipation of new business, spread throughout the community. The Cape May, Delaware Bay and Sewell's Point Railroad had gone bankrupt in 1916, and the line was sold for salvage on April 2, 1917. The construction of the new base gave part

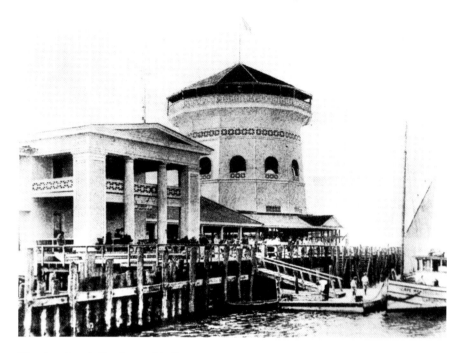

The abandoned "fun factory," built as an amusement center in 1912 on Sewell's Point, was chosen by the navy as temporary quarters for Cape May Section Base No. 9 after the United States entered the First World War. *H. Gerald MacDonald.*

of the 8.99-mile line a new lease on life. The government required a link from its base to the West Jersey and Seashore Railroad Station on Grant Street and assigned one hundred reservists to restore the line.

By July 1917, the old line had been put into service between the base and the iron pier in Cape May. The navy operated battery cars, as well as a small gasoline locomotive, to transport supplies and men. The line, known as the "Liberty Special" because one of its purposes was to transport navy personnel from the base to the city, survived until the end of the war.

Wissahickon Naval Training Barracks was constructed in 1917 on Henry Ford's property north of Schellinger's Landing. The papers reported that thousands of sailors filled Cape May's hotels and cottages, and the city constructed a new convention hall in 1917 to take advantage of the wartime prosperity. The Hotel Cape May was transformed into a naval hospital.

The Summer City by the Sea

The base was destroyed by a suspicious fire on July 4, 1918, while most of the base personnel marched in the Independence Day parade in the city. Temporary quarters were established, and the navy immediately constructed a new base.

The promising activity abated when the war ended. The Bethlehem Steel Company packed its bags and moved on, abandoning its munitions testing complex. Left behind was a deadly legacy: hundreds of "duds" (unexploded shells) buried on the Cape May beaches. Dozens of these shells proved to be live and killed and maimed many people for years after the war ended.

No longer required during peacetime, most of the Wissahickon Barracks was dismantled in 1919 and provided the lumber for a temporary postwar cottage boom. One of the camp buildings, an officers quarters, was moved and still stands today at the intersection of Columbia Avenue and Stockton Place. It was recently converted into a guesthouse. The naval base was taken over by the Coast Guard in 1925, and it became Coast Guard Section Base No. 9.

The January 1919 ratification of the Eighteenth Amendment to the Constitution that prohibited transportation and sale of alcoholic beverages had a major impact on Cape May. The isolated coastline along the Jersey Cape became a popular landing area for rumrunners intent on providing residents with demon rum while providing themselves with a profit.

The Coast Guard was charged with the unenviable task of enforcing the unpopular law. The government vessels—the *Kickapoo*, a 157-foot second-class cutter, and eighteen seventy-five-foot cutters (or "six-bitters") stationed at Section Base No. 9—waged an ongoing battle against the runners' well-financed operation.

Large ships from around the globe would lie offshore, just outside the government's jurisdiction, forming a "rum row" and awaiting the swift speedboats that would pick up the valuable cargo. Reports by bathers of offshore gun battles were common as the Coast Guard bravely fought the thankless war during the Prohibition era. With the exception of the airfield, Section Base No. 9 was abandoned by the Coast Guard at the end of prohibition in 1933.

Cape May began to use the slogan "Cool Cape May" as part of its advertising campaigns. The brochures read: "Surrounded on three sides by the open sea and the broad expanse of Delaware Bay, Cape May is cooled by refreshing sea breezes from almost every quarter. Its summer temperatures are consistently ten degrees cooler than those of surrounding areas." If the city was not as fashionable as Atlantic City, at least it was cooler.

The papers enthusiastically reported in February 1920 that Congress Hall, idle since 1908, was to be restored and "brought up in its appointments to the last minute of modern hotel perfection." The reporter promised that "[a]fter the summer season is over, it is planned to convert the hotel into a tropical palace, with its sunken gardens enclosed in glass filled with palms and tropical flowers, where the weird music of the Hawaiian orchestras will appeal to all lovers of the dansant."

As the hotel was being restored, more than three hundred men were busy constructing the largest hangar in the country (250 feet by 133 feet, with a 66-foot overhead) on the naval base grounds to house what newspapers referred to as "the big English blimp." Purchased by the government, the dirigible *ZR-2* was to arrive in Cape May and be housed in the new hangar that was completed in the early part of 1918.

Unfortunately, the airship crashed into the English Channel on its trial run, killing forty-four men on board, including a Cape May native. Interest in the hangar diminished after the tragedy, and the structure remained empty for years. It was later used by famed blimp designer Anton Heinan and eventually razed by the navy during a base restoration in 1941.

It took a new rumor and a scheme to fuel yet another land boom on the Jersey Cape. Everyone was aware that although the distance by highway between Cape Henlopen, Delaware, and Cape May Point was 170 miles, it was only 12 miles by water. Cape May was a dead-end at the southern tip of the peninsula. A reliable ferry service, a water highway connecting the South with the Jersey peninsula, would mean prosperity at last. Several attempts had been made over the years to establish a ferry, but most, including the Queen Anne Connection, ended in failure. The Queen Anne opened in 1900 but folded in 1904 due to its inability to establish a safe landing facility on the Jersey Cape.

In 1926, Jesse Rosenfeld, a Baltimore entrepreneur, was convinced that he had the answer to the transportation problem. He planned to purchase three World War I concrete ships and sink them to form a Y-shaped dock at Cape May Point, near the old steamboat landing site.

The Summer City by the Sea

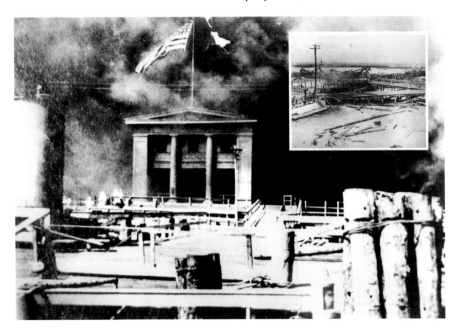

The suspicious "fun factory" fire of July 4, 1918, took place while most of the navy personnel were absent from the base, marching in the Independence Day parade in the city center. *Inset*: The aftermath of the fire that completely destroyed the old amusement center. *H. Gerald MacDonald.*

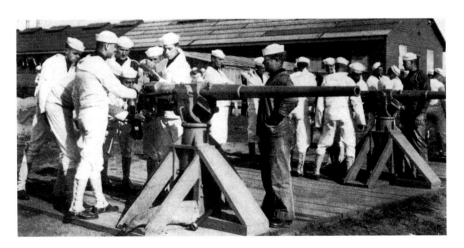

The Wissahickon Naval Training Barracks were located on Henry Ford's land near Schellinger's Landing. *H. Gerald MacDonald.*

He formed the National Navigation Company and purchased the *Atlantus*, one of four concrete ships constructed during World War I. The 250-foot-long *Atlantus* was wrestled from the mud of the James River in Virginia, where it had come to rest, and towed to Norfolk and then to Cape May, arriving on June 8, 1926.

The commander of the boat that towed the *Atlantus* from Norfolk stated that he had been delayed weeks by one mishap after another. As one writer noted, "This black, unbeautiful hulk represents the hopes of a million people on either side of the Bay."

Of the four concrete freighters built during the war, one had disappeared at sea, one was docked in Boston and the third was "doing service as a combination breakwater and hotel at Miami, Florida." It's amazing that as many as four of these monsters were constructed before the designers realized that making ships out of concrete was not a good idea.

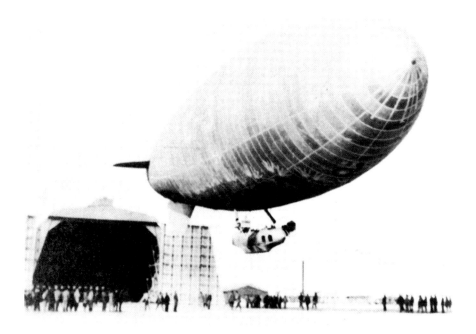

The Great Airship Hangar, constructed in 1918 on the naval base grounds, was the largest in the nation. Seen here is the Naval Air Station and blimp *C-3*. *H. Gerald MacDonald.*

The Summer City by the Sea

Anticipating this long sought-after connection with the South, investors began to purchase land in Cape May. A full-page advertisement in the *Cape May Star and Wave* promised that the Cape May boom had begun and that the new ferry would open in July 1926. Cape May hoped to draw guests from the metropolises of the South instead of relying exclusively on Philadelphia. The old Cape May Turnpike that connected the city with Rosenfeld's ferry site—the steamboat landing where the *Republic* and its ancestors once docked—was paved and renamed Sunset Boulevard. All available land between the city of Cape May and the proposed ferry landing was purchased by speculators and businessmen hoping to acquire a prime location along the route. The *Cape May Star and Wave* reported that "property values along the Boulevard have doubled and realtors declare that they will double again in price before reaching more nearly the real valuation under the new scheme of things."

A description of the *Atlantus* noted that "at present the hulk rides at her moorings awaiting the making of her final bed and is the object that draws hundreds of people every evening." Unfortunately, the *Atlantus* had a mind of its own concerning its final bed, and during a violent storm, it broke its mooring and promptly wedged itself in the sand forever. The ship is barely visible today from Sunset Beach, a monument to another scheme gone awry.

Rosenfeld's ferry project collapsed, and the memory of it discouraged many of his investors from attempting it again. Negotiations between the Delaware and New Jersey legislatures eventually resumed, but a common ground could not be reached and the ferry would not become a reality for another forty-three years.

As the ferry plan faltered, so did another scheme: the proposed consolidation of South Cape May, Cape May Point, West Cape May and Cape May City into Greater Cape May. The plan was supported by the Cape May City Progressive League, a civic organization formed in 1921 to improve and promote the resort. Proponents of the merger claimed that combining the four communities from "Harbor to the Bay" would create a "Florida of the North," with promises of the new Greater Cape May competing with hated rival Atlantic City. The voters did not share the vision, and the municipalities maintained their autonomy.

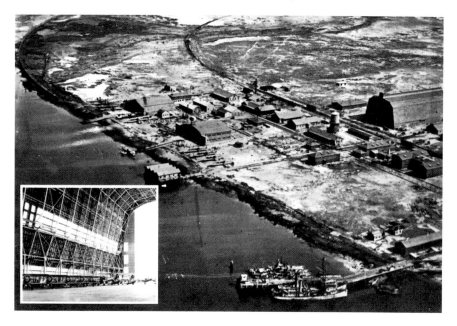

View of Naval Air Station Section Base No. 9, circa World War I, with airship hangar visible in upper right. *Inset*: Interior view of airship hangar, Section Base No. 9, with VJ5 planes stored inside. *H. Gerald MacDonald.*

The period between the 1926 failure of the Rosenfeld Cape May/Lewes Ferry scheme and the beginning of World War II was an uneventful era for the resort. One bright note was the completion of the Philadelphia and Camden Bridge (now the Ben Franklin Bridge) in 1926, but even this new connection with Philadelphia could not support the inflated land prices along the coast created by the dream of the ferry. Hundreds of lots went on the auction block, some selling for 1 percent of their land boom value.

The opening of the Benjamin Franklin Bridge and the convenience it provided automobile drivers headed for the Jersey shore signaled the death knell for the railroad era. By the time the bridge was opened, more people were traveling to the shore by automobile than by railroad. Improved roads in the Jersey peninsula increased truck and bus activity that further cut into the railroad's business. Finding it increasingly difficult to survive, the two competing railroads that once carried thousands of vacationers to the summer city by the sea merged in 1933, becoming the Pennsylvania-Reading Seashore Lines. (The new line survived until the

The Summer City by the Sea

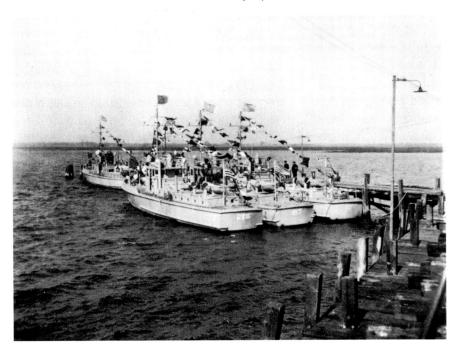

Coast Guard cutters stationed in Section Base No. 9. *H. Gerald MacDonald.*

bankruptcy of both parent companies, the Pennsylvania Railroad and the Reading, brought them under the control of Conrail in 1976.)

The Great Depression of the 1930s signaled an end to any hope that a major developer might step in to rescue the city.

The Coast Guard facility grew as more acreage was reclaimed by dredging, and the air strip was enlarged. The navy recommissioned the air station in September 1940 as the war in Europe escalated. In May 1942, the navy commissioned the Naval Base Cape May. The bankrupt Admiral Hotel (Hotel Cape May) was used by the navy as headquarters for the Delaware Task Force and later designated the U.S. Naval Annex. It housed officers and their dependents during the war.

The Coast Guard continued to maintain an antisubmarine station on the cape. The threat of enemy submarine activity off the Cape May peninsula was considerable. In March 1942, the U.S. Navy destroyer *Jacob Jones* was torpedoed and sunk by a German U-boat off Cape May. Only eleven men survived as the ship disappeared in less than thirty minutes. They were transported to the naval base by a rescue crew. (It is estimated

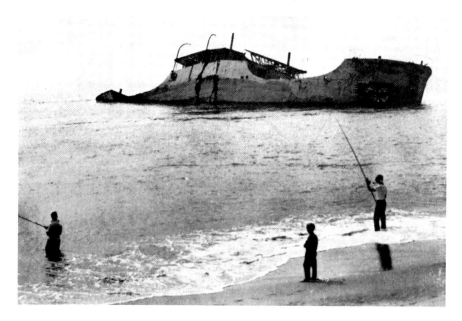

Atlantus imbedded in sandy grave after breaking mooring in ferocious storm. *Author's collection.*

that a minimum of ten ships were torpedoed within a mile of the Jersey coast during the war.)

Cape May complied with a required blackout and launched a massive public relations blitz to counteract the war-scare rumors that circulated throughout Philadelphia and other major cities. Officials who had just a few years earlier lobbied the military to recommission the base discovered that the location of the naval facility caused rumors to circulate that Cape May was now a primary military target. Another damaging tale was that the beaches were covered with "oil, bodies and barbed wire."

The city's mayor took exception with a *Time* magazine article entitled "War Time Living" and telegraphed the editor requesting a "correction." He wrote, "Your article creates false impressions which may do great damage to the tremendous seashore resort industry…we are patiently bearing all that is necessary to help win the war and can do without the publication of false rumors." He went on to say that the city was taking the coastal dim-out in the "usual sportsmanlike manner of Americans" and that the blue non-glare lights created a beautiful effect.

The Summer City by the Sea

The rumors did not abate, and it was reported that the Federal Bureau of Investigation would conduct an investigation to determine if "enemy agents were responsible for the false rumors."

Despite all of the city's public relations efforts, including the creation of a Cape May guide with the theme "V is for Victory and Vacations," gas rationing, material shortage and curtailed railroad service combined with the rumors to damage the resort industry. The Pennsylvania Railroad, the Reading Company and the Pennsylvania-Reading Seashore Lines announced in May 1942 that due to heavy government demands on the railroad for passenger car transportation, all one-day excursions between Philadelphia, Camden and the South Jersey coast resorts would be immediately discontinued. All nonessential building was also banned.

Panic concerning the U-boats caused the government to shut down the Cape May commercial fishing fleet. Cape May's popular senator I. Grant Scott protested the ban, claiming, "Fishermen in this area [are] precluded from the opportunity to earn their livelihood by the

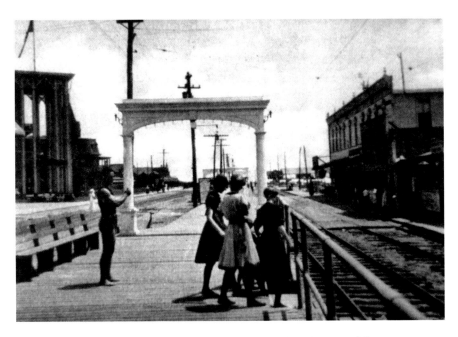

Early twentieth-century image of the Cape May boardwalk and a turn-of-the-century muscleman attempting unsuccessfully to capture the ladies' attention. The Lafayette Hotel is pictured on the left, and the trolley tracks are on the right. The lighted arches extended the entire length of the boardwalk until the early 1920s. *H. Gerald MacDonald.*

federal ban, which apparently was imposed as a result of rumors that boats in this area are supplying enemy submarines with fuel."

Unfortunately, all too many of the conservative Cape May City residents were quick to suspect the Italian and German American residents who populated the barrier island resorts just north of them of aiding the enemy.

The war did lead to the long-awaited construction of the Cape May Canal. The navy certified the canal as a primary emergency defense project in 1942, and this allowed the construction to take place at an accelerated pace. The work, most of which was completed by the U.S. Army Corps of Engineers, began in August 1942 and was completed in March 1943. The canal was used by the navy and Coast Guard during the war since it provided a protected shipping lane for military and commercial vessels traveling to and from Philadelphia.

V-E Day, on May 8, 1945, marked the end of the European phase of the war and the termination of the New Jersey coastal dim-outs. The navy relinquished the base to the Coast Guard the next year.

The Great Atlantic Hurricane

Although the nation was still at war, encouraging news from Europe had promoted a sense of optimism in Cape May throughout the summer season of 1944. Italy had fallen in May, and the Allied forces had made their historic landing in Normandy on June 6.

By August, American armored units had begun to move rapidly across France, and most Americans believed that victory was within their grasp. Although the dim-outs along the Jersey coast were still in effect, no U-boat attacks off the cape had been reported since December of the previous year. (This would eventually turn out to be the last attack off the coast.)

Cape May's commissioners were concerned about the continuing beach erosion problem since the remnants of a downgraded hurricane had struck the coast on August 1; the resulting high tide took a sizeable bite out of the famous Cape May beach. The erosion had accelerated since the construction of the Cold Spring jetties that were used to keep the Cape May harbor free of sand. In addition, Cape May and the tip of the peninsula had become an island again with the completion of the Cape May Canal, and some experts felt that the canal jetties were contributing to the substantial erosion of the beaches. The strand that had made the old resort famous was slowly washing out to sea.

As the city fathers discussed the merits of constructing a new jetty to protect the beach, nature was planning another surprise for Cape May

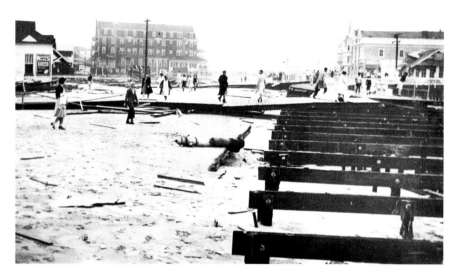

Beach Drive and a demolished boardwalk after the Great Atlantic Hurricane of 1944. The New Stockton Villa (now Macomber) is visible in upper left of photograph. *H. Gerald MacDonald.*

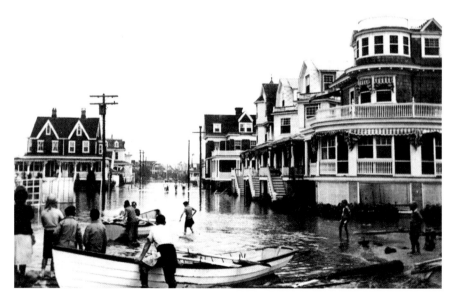

The storm surge temporarily transformed parts of the resort into a Venetian cityscape where rowboats became the preferred manner of transportation. *H. Gerald MacDonald.*

The Summer City by the Sea

City. It began its life as a tropical storm, growing in strength just east of Puerto Rico. Within a short period of time, the storm had developed into what the Weather Bureau in Miami dubbed the Great Atlantic Hurricane. By August 13, newspapers in Philadelphia had begun warning their readers that the dangerous storm was on its way and that there would be "a devil to pay." Prayers could not coax the furious tempest from its historic rendezvous with the Jersey coast.

As the U.S. Weather Bureau in Washington issued evacuation alerts for the residents of the North Carolina coast, the storm whipped winds of more than one hundred miles per hour. By 10:00 a.m. on September 14, the hurricane had turned slightly northeast after passing Cape Hatteras and picked up speed. The Coast Guard station hoisted the feared red and black hurricane flag.

By the time the storm reached Cape May, it was packing winds of fifty-five to sixty-three miles per hour with enough power to uproot trees and to inflict considerable structural damage on the city. Its calling card was a forty-foot storm surge that struck the resort just after 5:00 p.m. on September 14. The *Cape May Star and Wave* later described the towering wall of water, "with the northwest gale blowing back the high seas until they formed in a mountainous tidal wave, the full force of the mass of water was unleashed against the beach."

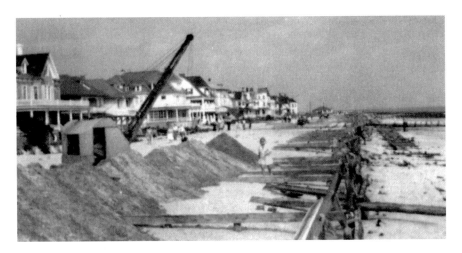

The city began the restoration of the beachfront immediately after the storm abated. Heavy equipment was needed to clear the tons of sand and debris that the storm had deposited on Beach Drive. *Cape May County Historical Society.*

The surge of water demolished the entire boardwalk, scattering sections of it as far as three blocks inland from the beach. The wooden walkway that had only a week before supported hundreds of vacationers was jettisoned by the tidal wave into cottages, hotels and commercial buildings. Most of the damage to the city was caused by airborne sections of the boardwalk.

The beachfront Convention Hall sustained considerable damage, and its fishing pier was torn away. The musical instruments that had recently been used to serenade ocean lovers were scattered everywhere. It was reported that the orchestra's baby grand piano was dumped into the Atlantic; pieces of it were later found as far as the Stockton Beach. Less than thirty feet of the Convention Hall's ballroom dance floor survived. The front of the ballroom along with most of the shops in the building escaped with only minor damage.

Severely damaged was the White House Tea Room, near the Convention Hall, along with the seaward ends of Hunt's Pier and the

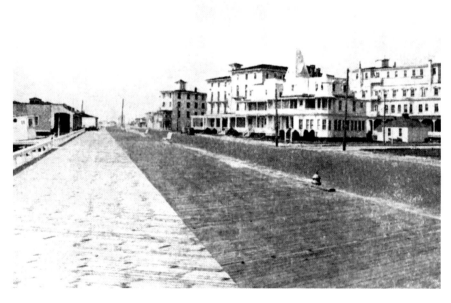

The city proudly published this photograph of the same scene six months after the storm to demonstrate to the public that the resort was again open for business. *Helenclare Leary*.

The Summer City by the Sea

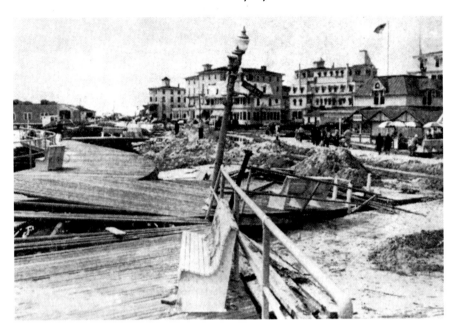

A September 15, 1944 photograph captures the total destruction of the boardwalk. The tidal wave jettisoned much of the boardwalk into nearby buildings, causing additional damage. *Helenclare Leary.*

Pennyland Pier. The understructure of all the piers was damaged, their pilings snapped and ripped by nature's terrible force. Beach Drive was impassable from end to end, covered with four feet of sand and debris.

The city mobilized immediately. The Red Cross Disaster Force, organized because of the war, jumped into action. Congress Hall, which had just closed for the season, reopened to provide care and shelter for the homeless. The Colonial, Lafayette and Columbia all assisted in the effort.

The hurricane washed out to sea the remnants of South Cape May. More than two hundred houses throughout Cape May City had sustained roof or chimney damage as the ninety-three-mile-per-hour winds ripped through the resort. A great loss was the destruction of more than two hundred trees that had been a source of pride for the city. The navy had saved its airplanes attached to the Cape May Naval Base by moving them to Lakehurst before the storm struck.

The city began clearing the wreckage and immediately rebuilding. A temporary fire lane was cleared through the sand on Beach Drive.

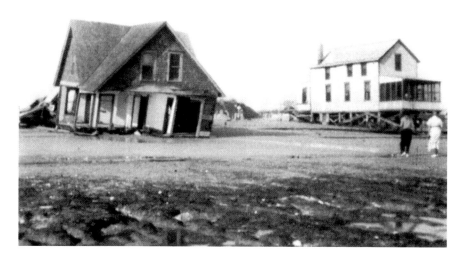

The 1944 hurricane sounded the death knell for the borough of South Cape May. The last remaining cottages were undermined by the hurricane. Years of storms had eroded most of the beachfront. The borough was officially dissolved one year later in 1945. *Richardson Collection/Cape May County Historical Society.*

Despite concern about obtaining sufficient labor and material due to the war, lumber was released to permit emergency repairs, and by the 1945 summer season, most of the storm's damage had been repaired, including the construction of a new boardwalk. An editorial in the *Cape May Star and Wave* on September 21, 1944, noted that "while most considerations paled into insignificance before the magnitude of the hurricane, a cheerful note in this hour of darkness was the recent disclosure that the ban on private building is expected to be removed with the collapse of Germany…the general relaxation of restrictions on private buildings will undoubtedly result in additional construction in Cape May."

Miraculously, the hurricane caused no loss of life in the city.

Peace and Preservation

The end of World War II signaled the start of an era of postwar prosperity throughout the nation. Builders and architects responded to a demand by returning soldiers for affordable housing by developing low-cost single-story homes. Cape May entered a new period of growth, with the emphasis on small, single-family dwellings. With the continuing decline in the resort industry in Cape May, no new hotels were needed. The last hotel to be built in the city had been the modest New Stockton Villa back in 1914 on part of the site of the old Stockton Hotel. The land between East Cape May and the old city center began to slowly fill in with homes.

In the 1950s, a major catalyst for growth in tourism and in the year-round population was the building of an important automobile thoroughfare. The New Jersey legislature gave the green light to a parkway, a toll road that would run south from the northern border of New Jersey to Cape May. This 173-mile asphalt ribbon joined the Jersey shore with the dense population centers of North Jersey and the New York metropolitan area. The final connecting link of the Garden State Parkway was completed in September 1954 and fueled the growth of the permanent population in the city and county of Cape May.

Lack of interest in the city prevented the wholesale destruction of the older structures. Columnist Paul Jones, writing for the *Philadelphia Evening Bulletin*, noted in 1955 that "they do not do much tearing down in Cape May, and that is one of its charms."

In 1958, four years after the final leg of the parkway was completed, historian John T. Cunningham attested to the city's condition by noting in his book *The New Jersey Shore* that "Cape May right now is relatively unspoiled—the consequence of being off the beaten path."

The following year, 1959, marked the 350th anniversary of Henry Hudson's 1609 journey that led to the first documented observation of the Jersey Cape and the Delaware Bay. The city planned a series of events to commemorate the voyage, including a water carnival, parade, horse show and costume (optional) inaugural ball held at Convention Hall on July 11, 1959. While local merchants benefited from the celebration, an editorial in the *Cape May Star and Wave* one month after the ball chastised the community for its apathy concerning Cape May's 350th anniversary. "The Silence was Eloquent," the editor noted, referring to a town meeting that was held to discuss the direction that the continuing celebration should take. Evidently, only 40 of the 1,200 citizens invited by special invitation had attended the meeting. The editorial surmised that the poor showing "left little doubt about the answer to the question, how far was the community willing to go…[apparently not very]. Maybe that's characteristic of small towns. Maybe, too, that's why they are and why they continue to be small towns."

What is significant about the 350th celebration is an idea that began to germinate in a few residents' minds as early as 1959. The editorial went on to prophetically note that the city might serve itself well to reemphasize its historic background.

An article that summer reminded citizens that the city's historic hotels played a large part in the resort's appeal. The author mentioned Congress Hall, the Windsor, the Chalfonte, the Colonial and the Lafayette, all built in the nineteenth century.

As the nation was captivated by the selection of its first astronauts, and Pan American World Airways initiated the first passenger service circling the globe, a few of Cape May's visionaries realized that there was a special value to the city that time had passed by. Preservationists rejoiced when the National Trust for Historic Preservation held its annual meeting at the resort in 1959. Local businessman Howard Tenenbaum called for the establishment of a municipal planning board to preserve Cape May's great historical heritage and establish long-range community plans. The mayor, Carl R. Youngberg, disagreed with Tenenbaum, stating his concern that

The Summer City by the Sea

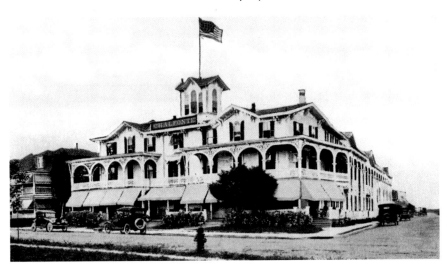

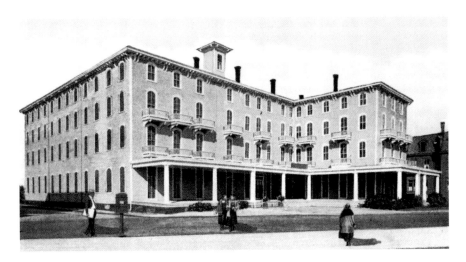

This page: The Chalfonte (above) and the Lafayette (below) were two of the hotels that were noted in a 1959 preservationist article. Visionaries began to slowly recognize the value of these older structures to the ailing resort. *Author's collection.*

"such a board would attempt to establish prohibitive regulations on new buildings" and dismissing the idea as being too expensive.

The lines were being drawn between the residents and officials who wanted to tear down and rebuild, the "ratables" as they became known, and those who wanted to preserve Cape May's architectural treasures.

Another visionary who recognized the commercial value of the city's structures, Dr. Irving Tenenbaum, chairman of the Historical and Preservation Committee of the Lower Cape May Regional Chamber of Commerce, championed the gaslight project, whose goal was to illuminate certain historic sections of the city. Tenenbaum noted that "the major purpose of the installation would be the historical preservation and restoration of specific areas…we have a distinct heritage of many examples of Victorian architecture in Cape May and our organization believes that this excellent historical background should be capitalized on." Tenenbaum and his committee convinced other service organizations of the significance of the gaslight project and collected written endorsements from fourteen groups. The mayor and commission eventually gave their approval. About fifty lights were purchased from the Welsbach Gaslight Company of Baltimore, Maryland, and installed by the New Jersey Natural Gas Company.

Special tribute should be given to Irving Tenenbaum as a "practical preservationist." He was one of the first residents of Cape May to realize that the historic architecture was a way to expand the resort's short summer season, extending it from early April to late October. This, in turn, shortened the off-season that benefited the

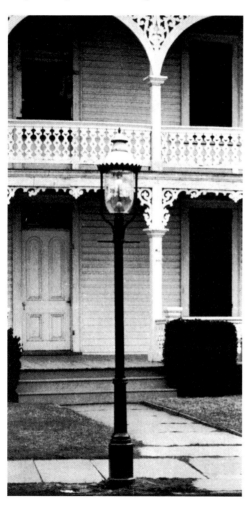

More than fifty vintage gaslights were purchased and installed. *Author's collection.*

economic situation. The county often experienced 19 percent unemployment during the off-season. A pragmatist, Tenenbaum would state years later that his own interest in Victorian architecture was its cash value, its potential to stimulate the local economy. He said, "[W]e have more and more and bigger and better motels here in Cape May to occupy our diminishing ground to entice more and more people to this same overused piece of ground for the same two months that have been coming for years and years…nothing had been done to improve our economic status." It would eventually take

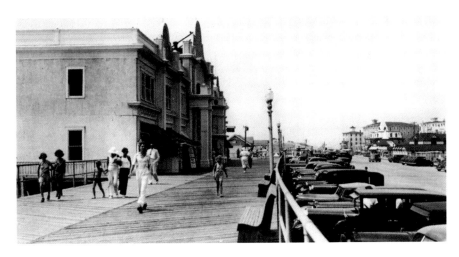

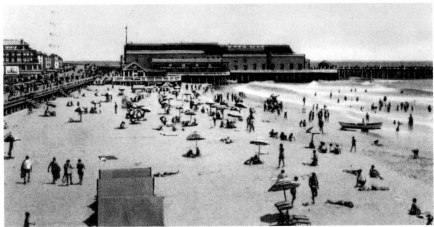

This page: Convention Hall and the boardwalk (top), circa 1940. Convention Hall and fishing pier (bottom), circa 1944. Community leaders recognized that Cape May's future lay in extending the traditional summer season. *Author's collection.*

a coalition of practical preservationists like Tenenbaum and architectural purists to improve the ailing resort.

As the 1960s approached, Cape May City was ripe for change. Many citizens were disenchanted with the hardball conservative Republican politics that had run the city for decades. A resident who lived in the city during the 1950s remembered that election irregularities were common and that anyone who crossed the small group that controlled the Republican stronghold could expect swift reprisals.

In 1960, attorney Walter C. Wright Jr. led a grass-roots movement to change the city's form of government from a commission to a three-man council/city manager format. Cape May had last operated under this type of government from 1924 to 1937. A petition signed by 559 residents forced a special referendum and served notice on the political machine of the voter unhappiness.

The politicians attempted an eleventh-hour maneuver to block the referendum by filing a taxpayer's suit in the New Jersey Superior Court. Wright waged a single-handed battle in both the state's Superior and Supreme Courts to ensure the survival of the referendum. The Supreme Court's decision to uphold an appeal against two Superior Court decisions to block the referendum was the first major political upset of the local Republican organization in years.

The voters overwhelmingly chose the new form of government. Wright polled the highest vote in the October 4 special election and was named mayor. Although Walter C. Wright Jr.'s revolution began as a tax revolt, the widespread dissatisfaction with the old regime prompted the reform mayor to tackle many of the city's mounting problems, and for the first time, the city was managed by a group that claimed to understand the significance of the resort's history.

The Winds of Change

Ironically, it was two disasters, one in the late nineteenth century and the second in the last half of the twentieth, that helped create the Cape May city that exists today.

The first, the Great Fire of 1878, presented the city with a thirty-five-acre canvas that conservative builders filled with equally conservative cottages and hotels. A time capsule of hundreds of Victorian structures built over a twenty-year span was an unexpected and fortuitous result of the conflagration. The second disaster occurred in early March 1962 in the form of a fierce northeaster that chewed up the New Jersey coast. The storm was unique in that it did not mount the full-fledged attack for which hurricanes were known but instead quietly mugged the coast, arriving unannounced and stealing centuries of history. The weather reports for Monday, March 5, predicted nothing out of the ordinary for a late winter day: "Monday: chance of rain, cloudy. Tuesday: cool and cloudy."

There were no advance warnings, no radio bulletins and no evacuation plans; no one saw the storm coming. Even the sun, the moon and the earth took part in the conspiracy. There was a new moon, a time of traditionally high tides, when the sun and moon are in alignment. Perigee tides, higher than normal tides that occur every six or seven months when the moon is at the closest point to the earth in its orbit, joined the gang.

Known as a northeaster, the storm was the sinister child of two weather systems—one a powerful snowmaker born in the Midwest,

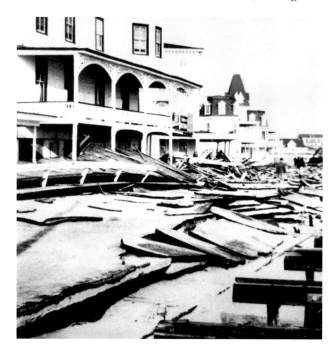

The March Storm of 1962 chewed up thirteen blocks of the boardwalk, spreading debris up and down Beach Drive. Denizot's Ocean View Cottage (now Maureen) is pictured in the upper left of photograph, and the Lafayette Cottage is shown in the upper right. *Cape May County Historical Society.*

traveling east to unite with its mate, a southern fire-eater forming off the coast of Georgia. The two joined and headed north to create havoc. The storm would have cut its visit to the Jersey coast short had it not been for another conspirator, an arctic cold front barreling down from Canada that stopped the monster in its tracks.

The northeaster stalled long enough to gather strength and then began battering the coast with between Force 10 and 11 winds; a mixture of rain, snow, sleet and hail; and twenty-five- to thirty-five-foot waves.

Cape May's already eroded beaches were in no shape to mount a defense. Witnesses later stated that they would have preferred the fury of a hurricane to this insatiable creature. The *Cape May County Gazette* reported, "[W]hile other storms may have equalled or surpassed this in peak intensity, few lasted as long or pounded the areas as unceasingly from the northeast."

This was no hit-and-run affair. The New Jersey coastal storm of the century, assisted by its accomplices, slowly and viciously pounded the coast for three days and nights. Each flood tide (seven in all) signaled another round of destruction, accompanied by fifty-five-knot winds.

The Summer City by the Sea

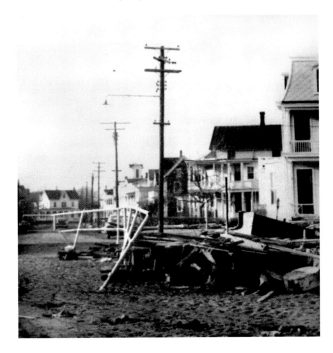

Seven devastating flood tides transformed the oceanfront into a scene that resembled a war zone. *Cape May County Historical Society.*

When the destroyer finally moved north, the sun illuminated its handiwork: a city in shambles. Thirteen blocks of Cape May City's fifteen-block boardwalk were demolished. Beach Drive, from end to end, was broken into a pile of black debris. Convention Hall was damaged beyond repair, and the city was flooded with as much as two feet of water. Water had entered the old bed of Cape Island Creek from the harbor and the canal, and a torrent of water had cut a wide gash along the creek's path, flooding the South Cape May meadows on its journey to the ocean. Cottages, hotels and commercial structures sustained costly damage as each new flood tide claimed another heating system, resulting in burst pipes and freezing buildings. The famous Cape May beach, the area's key to survival as a resort, had all but vanished.

The *Cape May Star and Wave* reported on March 8, 1962, that "Cape May stands today a stricken community...the cruelest blow ever dealt it by a rampaging sea as every high tide from early Monday through today [Thursday] inflicted greater and more devastating damage throughout the beachfront and in most sections of the city."

Since it was not a hurricane, the storm was never christened and remained nameless—anonymous destruction as a final insult. Yet many felt a need to name the destroyer. Some called it the Great March Storm, the Ash Wednesday Storm or just the Storm of the Century. One thing that everyone could agree on was that the Jersey coast had experienced nothing like it in its recorded history, a slap on the wrist from old Neptune for our arrogance in building too close to his dominion and a reminder of his awesome power.

"Putting More Christianity in the Patriots"

Shortly after the Great March Storm of 1962, Cape May was visited by another powerful force, fundamentalist minister Carl McIntire. He was the charismatic leader of the International Council of Christian Churches, pastor of the Bible Presbyterian Church of Collingswood, New Jersey, and editor of the influential *Christian Beacon Press*. He was also the director of the *Twentieth Century Reformation Hour* broadcast, which had more than four hundred station outlets in the United States and Canada.

With the Cape May/Lewes Ferry scheduled to begin operation within the next year, Cape May would finally shake its "dead-end" status. (The opening day ceremony took place on June 30, 1964.) McIntire recognized the resort's new potential and became smitten with the feeling of Americana that the aging resort evoked. A major tenet of his ministry was his widely publicized anticommunist crusades. What better place to set down roots than America's oldest seaside resort? His motto said it all: "Putting More Christianity in the Patriots and more Patriotism in the Christians."

McIntire began to purchase properties in Cape May and, in a short time, was one of the resort's major landowners. Among his acquisitions were Congress Hall, the Windsor Hotel, the Virginia Hotel and the vacant Admiral Hotel. (The Admiral was the old Hotel Cape May.) He immediately changed the name of the Admiral to the Christian Admiral and dedicated it on May 30, 1963 as the Reformation Center of the Twentieth Century.

The hotel provided rooms for the faithful, as well as conference facilities where McIntire's followers could attend weeklong seminars featuring prominent religious and conservative celebrities such as Senator Strom Thurmond of South Carolina and evangelist radio preacher Dale Crowley. The third floor of the hotel was set aside as the "Hall of the States," with rooms assigned to each state. The minister contacted each state government requesting that it furnish and decorate its room in accordance with what was distinctive and representative of the state's life and history. The cost was $1,000 per room. He announced that Pennsylvania, Virginia, New York and New Jersey had acquired "state" rooms. McIntire planned to originate some of his *Twentieth Century Reformation Hour* broadcasts from the Christian Admiral during the summer season.

His next step was to relocate Shelton College, the Christian-oriented Ringwood, New Jersey college, to Cape May. To accommodate the school, McIntire began to purchase and move several more buildings to the Christian Admiral site. He provided the city with a spectacle in October 1963 when he moved the two Lafayette Hotel cottages, originally located at Ocean and Beach, to his Trenton Avenue property. The city watched in amazement as the two cottages were slowly transported down Beach Drive, with McIntire broadcasting his radio show from the front porch of one of the buildings.

This was not the first time the cottages had been moved; they began life as one building, the Weightman cottage, originally located on the corner of Franklin and Washington Streets, site of the Cape May Post Office. Built before the Civil War for Philadelphian chemist William Weightman Sr., the summer cottage was moved to the Ocean and Beach Drive site in 1881 when Weightman's son decided that an ocean view would be pleasant. Legend states that he hired local farmers to move the house, and upon discovering that it was too large to move in one piece, they cut it in half. The two sections were slowly moved by man and mule power, but upon arriving at the site, the locals discovered that they could not join the building back together. The summer season was quickly approaching, and so was Mr. Weightman, so they enclosed the sides of each "cottage" and returned to their farms. The two structures have remained separate for over a century. They are currently restored and used as a popular bed-and-breakfast.

The Summer City by the Sea

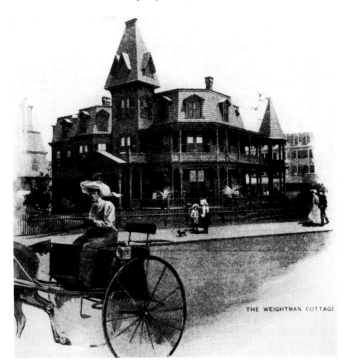

The Lafayette Hotel cottages began life as the Weightman Cottage, which was originally located on the corner of Franklin and Washington Streets. *H. Gerald MacDonald.*

Carl McIntire also purchased and moved the Morning Star/Evening Star Villa from Ocean Street to a vacant lot near the Christian Admiral. The Evening Star was eventually demolished to accommodate the automobile; the Morning Star survives today as a condominium complex.

McIntire offered to move the historic Lafayette Hotel before its demolition in 1970, but the city claimed that it was concerned about Beach Drive's ability to withstand the enormous weight, and the hotel fell prey to the bulldozer.

Shelton College prospered for a short time, boasting a two hundred plus student enrollment, but then it all came to an end. The conservative school lost its accreditation from the State of New Jersey, and after a futile legal battle, McIntire moved the college to Florida. His ministry was dealt another blow when the Federal Communications Commission revoked his broadcast license in 1973. The flamboyant minister again entered into a battle and again lost. Local residents remember how his *Radio Free America* was defiantly broadcast off the New Jersey coast from an old World War II minesweeper.

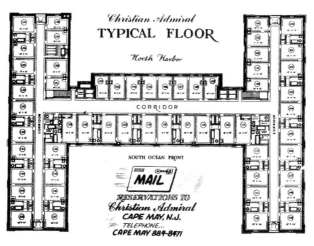

Illustration of floor plan (above) of Christian Admiral published in the Christian Beacon Press. (below) McIntire's future Christian Admiral (Hotel Cape May) as it appeared in 1943. (Author's collection)

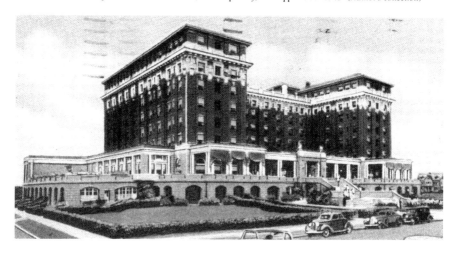

Illustration of floor plan (top) of the Christian Admiral, published in the *Christian Beacon Press*. McIntire's future Christian Admiral (Hotel Cape May) as it appeared in 1943 (bottom). *Author's collection.*

McIntire's problems did not end there. He battled the City of Cape May in an attempt to obtain tax-exempt status for his many holdings and lost. The *Christian Beacon Press* filed for Chapter 11 bankruptcy in 1990. The company was millions of dollars in debt, and the City of Cape May was owed $750,000 in back taxes. There seemed to be no hope for the aging Christian Admiral and Congress Hall, both owned by the bankrupt company and in need of restoration. Two of McIntire's grandchildren stepped in and brokered a deal with their creditors that would eventually doom the Christian Admiral in order to save Congress Hall.

The Virginia Hotel (Ebbitt House) was sold to the Chamberlain Hospitality Group, headed by a McIntire relation. The historic structure was painstakingly restored and is today a popular restaurant and hotel. Many of McIntire's real estate holdings in East Cape May have been sold and developed over the last twenty years.

The reverend and his ministry have been a part of Cape May for more than three decades. Love him or hate him, no one can deny that the city owes him a debt of gratitude for his role as conservator. As a Cape May preservationist leader noted in a 1975 interview, "One of our allies was the Reverend Carl McIntire, the right-wing minister. He's for everything that's American, he says, and preserving old buildings is American." Reverend Carl McIntire died in 2002 at the age of ninety-five.

The City Is the Project

Everything Old Is New Again

While there was no shortage of opinions as to where Cape May's future lay after the Great March Storm of 1962, everyone agreed that the city needed help. In the past, there had always been a savior that seemed to appear in the city's darkest hours. This time, there was no railroad to spur a new boom and no syndicate of developers willing to invest in the old city by the sea.

The jet age offered Americans myriad vacation choices. Cape May was about to slip into oblivion. The once-famous beaches had all but disappeared, and a film of decay covered many sections of the city. Both state and federal funds would be needed to turn the resort around. This was the '60s, a time when almost everyone believed that there was no problem that the government could not solve.

The question was what direction the city would take. Would preservation become the jewel in the renewal crown, or would government funds be used to build what one architectural historian referred to as a sideshow on piles?

As time passed, more and more citizens believed that preservation was the key to the resort's future. In July 1962, a conference of historical administrators was held in Williamsburg, Virginia. A featured report of the event was given by Clemson College assistant professor of architecture Harold Norman Cooledge Jr. The *Cape May Star and Wave* reprinted his report one month later under the heading "Expert Sees Cape May's Future Tied to Exploiting Its Past."

The Summer City by the Sea

Cooledge's theory was that the city could materially improve its financial condition by rehabilitating its collection of mid-nineteenth century structures. He cautioned the city that a carbon copy of Wildwood (with boisterous bars and a circus-type boardwalk) was not the answer and advised Cape May citizens that they were "sitting on a goldmine...the most complete in situ grouping of mid-nineteenth century buildings east of the Mississippi." What was needed was an effort by the preservationists to convince the merchants and city fathers that the answer was not to tear down their most precious assets.

The concept of the city as a living classroom was taking shape. Cooledge prophetically warned the planners of a Victorian village that urban renewal was a powerful genie that "should be touched with a cautious hand." He had witnessed the product of bulldozer planning in cities throughout the country.

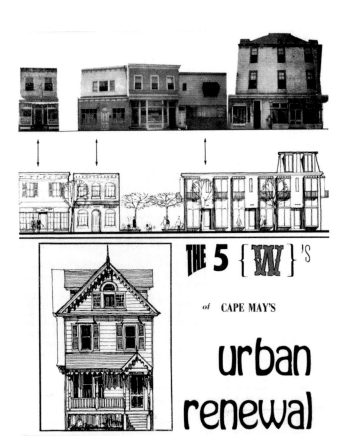

The city promoted the urban renewal project with the publication of the "5 W's of Cape May's Urban Renewal," complete with architectural before and after views. *Helenclare Leary.*

Encouraged by local resident Dr. Tenenbaum and Bill Murtagh, head of the National Trust in Washington, D.C., the city's administration applied for and received a federal grant from the Urban Renewal Administration in December 1963 to create Victorian Village, a restored nineteenth-century resort that would extend the traditional two-month summer season by offering tourists an alternative to the beach. In 1965, President Lyndon B. Johnson created his cabinet-level Department of Housing and Urban Development (HUD), which superseded the Urban Renewal Administration.

A local urban renewal office was established in city hall, and the town fathers promised Cape May "a bonanza of improvements…not just a restored village, but street improvements, storm sewers and downtown revitalization…all impossible with purely local funds."

A brochure explaining the project, *The 5 W's of Cape May's Urban Renewal*, was distributed to the citizens. In short, Cape May would benefit from the $2.9 million program at a cost of only $100,000 to the city, as well as from profit from the "Victorian Village destined to attract hundreds of thousands of American and foreign tourists."

Attracting all these tourists would be relatively easy compared to the parking problem this bonanza would create. Cape May was not a city designed with the automobile in mind, and the railroad system had slowly deteriorated over the years. The Pennsylvania-Reading Seashore Lines had begun curtailing unprofitable passenger service after World War II and each new summer season witnessed less service. The last passenger train arrived in Cape May on October 2, 1981. The city's restoration plans had to center on the automobile.

Another problem entailed how to prevent the Atlantic Ocean from paying another surprise visit to the city. Federal, state and city funds were used to address this problem. A $1 million masonry seawall—or promenade, as the romantics among us prefer to call it—was constructed. It has yet to be challenged by anything like the 1962 storm, and so far it has done the job. In addition to the wall, a series of jetties was constructed to preserve the beach.

The change in Cape May's beachfront would be nothing short of radical. The two largest hotels, Congress Hall and the Windsor Hotel, had their massive lawns turned into parking lots. (The Windsor burned to the ground in a suspicious fire in 1979.) The old Lafayette Hotel was demolished in 1970 and replaced with a new hotel that could accommodate parking. The Baltimore Inn was also demolished and replaced by a modern building with underground parking.

The Colonial escaped the wrecking ball when owner Ray Fite added a fifty-room motor lodge beside the old hundred-room hotel on the site where the Stockton Bath Houses once stood. The Star Villa was moved to provide a parking lot for the Colonial. The Lafayette Hotel's two cottages were saved when Carl McIntire moved them to his east Cape May site and a new motel was erected where they once stood. The Convention Hall that had been left dangling in the Atlantic after the 1962 storm was replaced.

The old railroad station that had stood between Washington and Lafayette Streets was razed to accommodate a massive parking lot attached to a supermarket and a small strip mall.

A centerpiece in the HUD project was the $3.8 million Washington Street pedestrian mall completed in 1971. The mall was created by closing Washington from Perry Street to Ocean Street. The street was torn up to allow underground wires, cables and gas and water lines to be installed and then landscaped into a comfortable pedestrian walk. Streets were opened behind the mall shops to replace the closed thoroughfare and provide parking.

As the urban renewal plan proceeded, two factions began to emerge in the city. The first, the preservationists, believed that the Victorian Village boundaries should be expanded until the entire city was restored to its former glory. The second group, the ratables, saw the urban renewal program more as an urban removal opportunity to tear down the old and fill the city with modern, air-conditioned motels and parking lots. For example, Henry Needles, whose family owned the Lafayette Hotel for almost fifty years, argued that the old hotel had to go because of insurance problems and a change in the public's taste, noting that the people his mother had served were dying out. A new facility with heat, air conditioning and a pool was needed to please the increasingly demanding tourist. It began to look like the ratables would have their way.

The *Cape May Star and Wave* warned the city in an editorial, "Officials here will tell you that the purpose of the Urban Renewal program was not so much to preserve the city's Victorian architecture as it was to stimulate its ratables, economy and growing power...it seems that the citizens of Cape May as a whole do not really appreciate the fine Victorian architecture which is found here." The city seemed ratable crazy, and at the pace buildings were falling to the developers' wrecking crews, Cape May would soon be the nation's oldest seashore resort in name only. Cape May was on the fast track to becoming a city of new "Victorian style" motels and shops—a Victorian Disneyworld.

The Eldridge Johnson house, known today as the Pink House (it's painted a bright shade of pink), was moved from its Congress Place location to Perry Street to accommodate a "Victorian" motel. Preservationists were incensed when the city gave the Catholic Diocese of Camden, New Jersey, the go-ahead to replace a sizeable chunk of the commercial district on Washington Street with a 205-unit high-rise senior citizens complex, which was baptized as Victorian Towers.

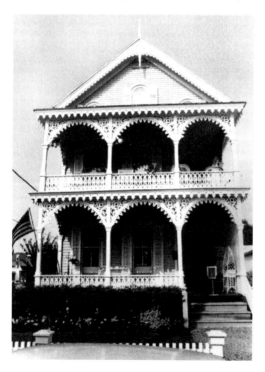

The Eldridge Johnson House (Pink House) was moved from Congress Place to Perry Street to accommodate a motel. *Photo by Emil R. Salvini.*

Part of the preservationists' dilemma was that the original urban renewal grant was applied for by reformer Walter Wright Jr. and his administration. By the time the money started to arrive, the city had voted in a new group, and it was unclear how it felt about historic preservation. A stone in its shoes and a champion of old Cape May quickly surfaced.

The federal money did not come without strings, and one urban renewal requirement was that a qualified architectural historian had to be hired to catalogue the buildings in the grant area. (Another requirement was that a Historic District Commission had to be created.) Enter Carolyn Pitts. With her background in the arts and architectural history, she tackled her assignment with a religious zeal. Had the ratable crowd known of her twenty-year love affair with the city by the sea, they would have seen to it that she was never hired. She later said, "I've been going down to Cape May ever since the '40s when I was a graduate student at Penn. It was cheap, it was deserted, and it was a big textbook of Victorian style."

Pitts was not surprised to discover that many of the city's full-time residents simply did not realize that the buildings were unique and historic. They felt that they were eyesores, fires just waiting to happen, and they envied their motel-ridden neighbors to the north. Pitts later reminisced in a 1993 *Smithsonian* article, "I hadn't realized what I was getting into…I was messing up their real estate game."

Pitts, or "Miz Pitts," as residents referred to her, spearheaded a group of summer residents and local leaders in the war to save Cape May's character (the Battle of Cape May, as she later named it). She catalogued an ever-expanding area, and in 1970, in a move that will be

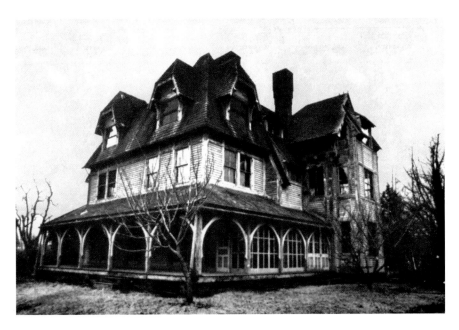

The Emlen Physick Mansion resembled a haunted house when the Mid-Atlantic Center for the Arts was organized to rescue it. *Cape May County Historical Society.*

forever remembered, she along with Cape May Cottagers Association preservation committee member Edwin C. Bramble managed to get the entire town listed on the federal government's National Register of Historic Places without the approval or knowledge of the city's mayor, Frank A. Gauvry; its congressman, Charles Sandman; or its governor, William T. Cahill.

Pitts later noted, "We sneaked it past them…we had to. It was register the town, or see it leveled and turned into another seashore honky-tonk… none of the buildings can be destroyed if you're using federal money." Once the deed was done, she notified the powers-that-be, offering them the opportunity to announce the honor to the public. The preservationists waited months, but no announcement came. Apparently, Congressman Sandman was attempting to have the federal designation overturned. His efforts were in vain. The Pitts faction grew tired of waiting for the

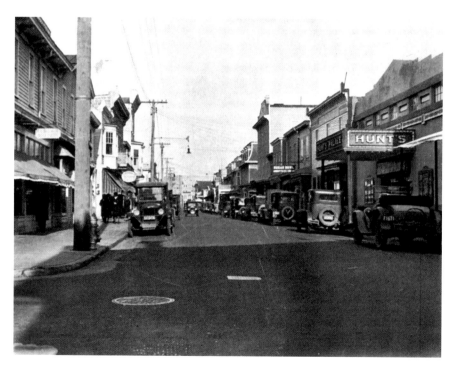

Above and next page: Sixty years of change. Washington Street taken from Perry Street looking east in 1927, 1958 and 1990. *Isaac B. Zwalley, 1927/1958; H. Gerald MacDonald, 1990.*

The Summer City by the Sea

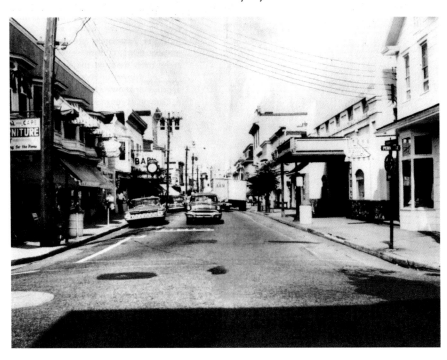

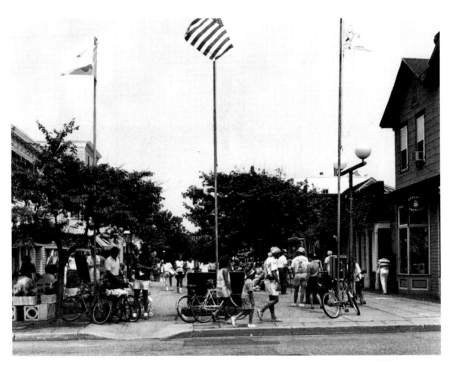

announcement and leaked the news to the *Philadelphia Bulletin*. Sandman announced it the following day, explaining that he had just been notified.

A spokesperson for the New Jersey Department of Environmental Protection issued a statement explaining why the honor was granted to the city: "There were several criteria categories, but the most important thing which gave it its unity was, of course, the style of Victorian architecture. It's one of the best, if not the best, single unified area of Victorian architecture in the state, if not the country." The designation protected the city from being encroached on by federally funded, licensed or authorized projects. This gave the preservationists some breathing room, time to convince the city's merchants that they had something worth saving. Pitts's end-run would be impossible today since as of 1981, secretaries of the interior will not designate buildings or districts as landmarks unless the owners unanimously consent.

The ratables had not given up. The same issue of the *Cape May Star and Wave* (January 28, 1971) that announced the historical designation also reported on the dissolution of the local Historic District Commission headed by preservationist Dr. Irving Tenenbaum. The May 6, 1971 *Cape May Star and Wave* reported that the mayor threatened to sue "the individuals responsible (without naming them) for the city's designation as a National Historic Site which in turn threw a monkey wrench into their plans."

In the meantime, another battle was ensuing. The Mid-Atlantic Center for the Arts was formed in 1970 to help save the Emlen Physick Mansion, Cape May's finest Victorian house. The city had promised to use HUD money to save the estate but later reneged. Pitts and summer resident Ed Bramble arranged for federal and state grants to assist the city in acquiring the estate. The plan was that the Mid-Atlantic group would raise the money to maintain the mansion so the city would not be saddled with the burden. The mayor and the ratable faction refused to accept the grant. They felt that the property was outside of the Victorian Village and too valuable for public use.

It seems that the administration did not correctly file the papers necessary to refuse the grant. Their action to turn down the money helped rally the preservationists, who gained control of the city government in the next election, with their leader, network television director and full-time resident Bruce Minnix, becoming mayor. He proudly attests to the fact that his first official act as mayor was to accept the Physick grant, and his last act in 1976 was to accept the designation of National Historic Landmark. This designation was a step higher than the original honor, and with it Cape May joined some select company: the Alamo, Texas, and Williamsburg, Virginia. The Physick Mansion was sold to the City of Cape May with a stipulation that it be leased to the Mid-Atlantic Center for the Arts.

Minnix lost his bid for reelection, but by the time the new administration took office in 1977, the concept and the commercial benefits associated with the "Nation's Oldest Seaside Resort" had become part of the community's fabric.

Renaissance

Over the next twenty-five years, the old resort experienced a rebirth. In what might be called the rise and fall and rise again of an American seaside village, Cape May rode a roller coaster through two hundred years of good and bad times, emerging as the nation's premier ocean retreat.

Now that the preservationists had saved more than six hundred examples of Victorian architecture, what was to become of them? The United States government listed them on an exclusive register, but someone had to give these privately owned buildings another reason to exist. Most were too large to maintain as private residences. The answer presented itself in the form of the American entrepreneur, a twentieth-century innkeeper who changed the city's destiny with hammers and paintbrushes. An enterprising bunch of visionaries with nothing in common but their love of Cape May and the sea, they bet the farm that lovers of the Victorian city would love to stay in a restored Victorian inn and won.

Renting rooms in Cape May was not a new concept, but for the first time in its history, it became fashionable. The new breed of innkeepers came from diverse backgrounds. A retired chemist, a network television director, a psychologist and a Coast Guard officer were all willing to invest their sweat equity in a dream. Some were tired of the rat race; others sought to fulfill a secret desire to own their own businesses. The names they chose for their inns and guesthouses were as varied as their backgrounds: the Abbey, Holly House, Victorian Lace and the Mainstay. As these first inns became successful, more believers followed. Eventually, more Victorians came alive

The Summer City by the Sea

as inns, restaurants and shops. The colorful quilt that is Cape May took shape. Today, there are more than fifty bed-and-breakfast lodgings in the city.

The Mid-Atlantic Center for the Arts (MAC), housed in the beautifully restored Emlen Physick Mansion, serves as a cultural hub for the community, offering a variety of programs and conducting walking and trolley tours throughout the year. It has helped lengthen the traditional season from Memorial Day to Labor Day with events such as the Victorian Weekend, Historic District Trolley Tours and the Mansions by the Sea Tour. When this book was first written, MAC had vowed to never succumb to ghost tours. After watching a score of independent operators walk eager visitors through the village, pointing out "haunted" homes on the gaslit streets, MAC embraced the specters and the much-needed funds. Today, it is the leading ghost tour operator in Cape May, with a wide choice of apparition tours by foot or trolley. It is all harmless fun, and there are now more than seventy

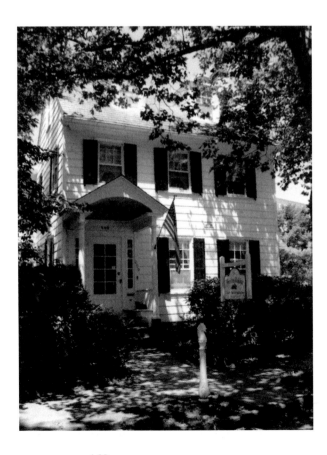

A new breed of entrepreneurs transformed dozens of historic homes into profitable bed-and-breakfasts. *Photo by Emil R. Salvini.*

events in Cape May between February and December. It is the only resort along the Jersey coast that has successfully extended its season.

Cape May won the battle with its numerous competitors and did it with style. The mansions of Newport survive today only as museums, tributes to the Gilded Age, and they owe their existence to the Preservation Society of Newport County. The world-renowned old hotels of Atlantic City and Long Branch have fallen prey to progress and the wrecking ball. Legalized gambling has changed the face of Atlantic City, and traditional beachfront hotels have been replaced with high-rise waging palaces. Although more than a century has elapsed since Atlantic City began its competition with Cape May, they continue to attract dissimilar tourists. Cape May is still a favorite with families and traditionalists, while Atlantic City continues to cater to the faster crowd.

Cape May, the summer city by the sea, has persevered and regained the title of "Queen of the Seaside Resorts." A success story, yes, but not without its challenges. A parking spot during peak season is a rare find, and many bed-and-breakfast lodgings are unable to accommodate their guests' vehicles. Because summer cottages constructed during the horse

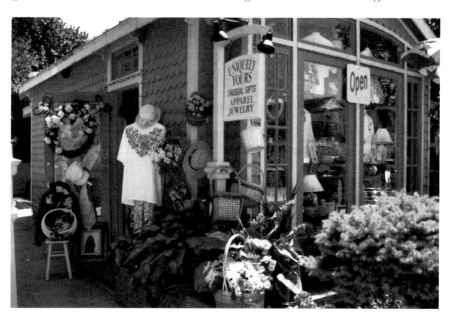

The bed-and-breakfast renaissance was followed by the creation of scores of quaint shops and restaurants throughout the historic district. *Photo by Emil R. Salvini.*

The Summer City by the Sea

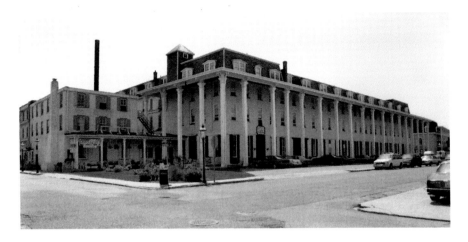

Congress Hall shops occupy the first floor of the old hotel. *Photo by Mark Henninger/ImagicDigital.com.*

and carriage era had no need for driveways, many buildings are separated by only a few feet. Parking and traffic were major concerns when this book was originally written, and the problem remains. Options ranging from satellite parking regions serviced by shuttle buses to passenger rail service into the city are being considered. The more that out-of-towners discover the resort, the more congested the city becomes.

A conflict has developed between a city government that has grown to depend on the resort's plentiful parking meters and parking fines as a source of income and the tourists who feel victimized by them. The city is patrolled during the summer by an army of meter persons that is excessively vigilant and rigid. The business community fought for the tourist trade in 1994 by experimenting for nine days in July with an "angel" program—volunteers roamed the city, pumping quarters in expired meters in an effort to assist tourists in avoiding stiff fines. The city was not pleased with the loss of revenue and put a stop to it.

On the preservation front, the Historic Preservation Commission (the Commission, or HPC) won a battle when the city passed an ordinance allowing it to bypass the planning board when making recommendations on historic structures.

HPC is responsible for maintaining the Victorian standards of the city. It is often accused of playing politics or being inconsistent in interpreting the official City of Cape May's Design Standards, but these volunteers

Historic Cape May, New Jersey

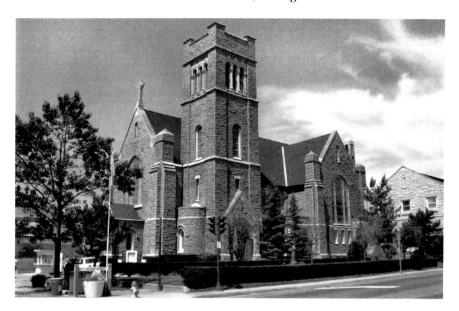

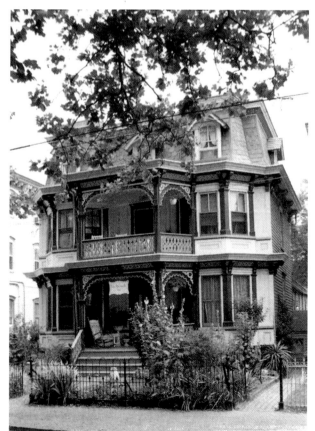

Above: Our Lady Star of the Sea, Roman Catholic Church (1911), located on the mall, is a favorite of tourists and residents. *Photo by Emil R. Salvini.*

Left: The George Hildreth Cottage (1882), located on Jackson Street, has been meticulously restored and is today a charming bed-and-breakfast. *Photo by Emil R. Salvini.*

The Summer City by the Sea

are all that exist between the Victorian summer city by the sea and the wrecking ball. The larger historic buildings are the most problematic since they are expensive to maintain and operate. The Christian Admiral and Congress Hall were both in desperate need of restoration when the company that owned them, the *Christian Beacon Press*, declared bankruptcy in 1990. Both properties appeared doomed when a painful but practical plan was born. The Christian Admiral was demolished in 1996, and in return, the owners pledged to restore Congress Hall with the revenue from the sale of the property where it once stood. Congress Hall has been carefully restored, and seaside mansions now stand on the footprint of the venerable Christian Admiral (or Hotel Cape May).

Erosion is a never-ending problem, and the once great Cape May strand will never return to its former glory. Nineteenth- and early twentieth-century visitors to the seaside village wrote postcards describing walking hundreds of feet out to sea on a sloping ocean bottom only to find themselves waist high in the refreshing, gentle surf.

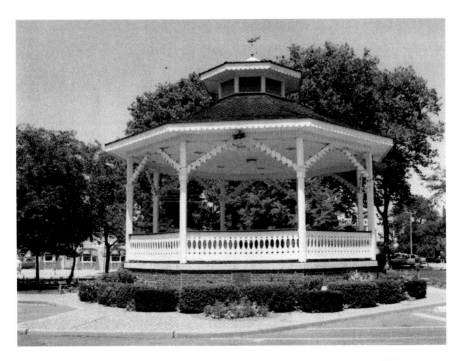

The bandstand in Rotary Park is the site of the summer concert series. *Photo by Emil R. Salvini.*

Historic Cape May, New Jersey

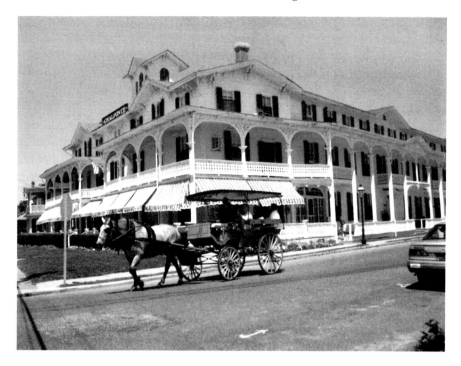

A popular way to tour the summer city by the sea is by horse and carriage. The Chalfonte Hotel (1875) was one of the three hotels to survive the Great Fire of 1878. The other two were the Baltimore House (1870), 642 Hughes Street, and the Arlington Hotel (1878), Grant and North Streets. *Photo by Emil R. Salvini.*

The City of Cape May has a long-term commitment from the federal government to maintain the beaches. An eternal battle against nature rages on, with recent storms claiming some of the newly restored beaches on the western end of town. Beach replenishment is on the calendar, but even with these programs, man-made obstructions in the natural sand flow have reduced the once-famous strand to a shadow of its former self and inadvertently benefited its neighbor to the north. The local joke is that if you want to know where Cape May's beaches have gone, go to Wildwood. Anyone who has walked from Wildwood's boardwalk to the ocean at low tide can verify this theory. Cape May's future depends on the combined drawing card of the ocean and its primary attraction, the living Victorian cityscape. Few seaside towns possess such a resource—hundreds of quaint, handcrafted cottages situated on tree-lined streets, with the Atlantic providing the backdrop.

The Summer City by the Sea

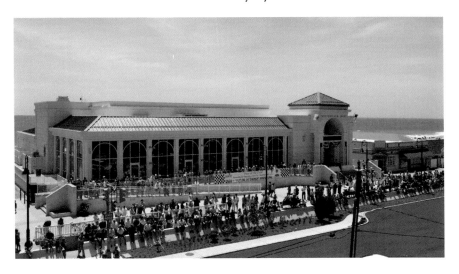

On May 25, 2012, Memorial Day weekend, the city proudly celebrated the opening of the new twenty-thousand-square-foot Convention Hall. This current structure is the third Cape May Convention Hall and can accommodate up to one thousand people for performing arts concerts and six hundred people for weddings, seminars, banquets and, naturally, conventions. *Cape Publishing Inc.*

In May 2012, the City of Cape May proudly dedicated its new Convention Hall, replacing the smaller structure that was constructed after the Great Atlantic Storm of 1962. The new hall, located on the seaside promenade, is designed to accommodate more than nine hundred people for events including conventions, concerts, tradeshows, banquets and meetings.

In October 2012, an unprecedented "superstorm," Hurricane Sandy, decimated the New Jersey coastline and lower New York City. While Cape May was predicted to be ground zero, the storm traveled slightly north just before making landfall and spared the venerable resort. While towns like Seaside Heights and Long Beach Island were unrecognizable after Sandy, Neptune forgave the Summer City for building too close to his lair.

The summer city by the sea owes its rebirth to the small group of visionaries that recognized the value of its architecture as a means to extend the resort's traditionally short summer season. The worth of the fragile resource can be diminished, however, by inaccurate restorations, haphazard removal of vintage structures and the addition of garish pseudo-Victorian commercial enterprises. Citizens and elected officials must be sensitive to the fact that while no one building is of major historic significance, they all combine to create the Cape May experience.

BIBLIOGRAPHY

Alexander, Robert Crozer. *Ho! For Cape Island.* N.p.: Edward Stern & Company, 1956.

———. *Light of Asia.* Fifteenth Annual Bulletin, Cape May Geographic Society, Cape May, New Jersey, June 1961.

Bailey, John. *Sentinel of the Jersey Cape: The Story of the Cape May Point Lighthouse.* Cape May, NJ: Mid-Atlantic Center for the Arts, 1989.

Barber, John W., and Henry Howe. *Historical Collections of the State of New Jersey.* Newark, NJ: Benjamin Olds, 1844.

Beitel, Herbert M., and Vance C. Enck. *Cape May County: A Pictorial History.* Norfolk/Virginia Beach, VA: Donning Company, 1988.

Blumenson, John J. *Identifying American Architecture.* New York: W.W. Norton & Company, 1977.

A Book of Cape May. Cape May, NJ: Albert Hand Company, 1937.

Boyer, George F., and J. Pearson Cunningham. *Cape May County Story.* Avalon, NJ: Avalon Publishing Company, 1975.

Bruce Minnix, interview by author, 1992.

Cape Island Historical Celebration Committee. *Historical Diary of Cape Island.* Cape May, NJ: self-published, 1964.

Cape May, Old and New. Cape May, NJ: Pennsylvania Railroad, 1912.

Cape May Real Estate Company brochure, Cape May, New Jersey, 1903.

Cook, Joel. *Brief Summer Rambles Near Philadelphia.* Philadelphia, PA: J.B. Lippincott & Company, 1882.

Bibliography

Cunningham, John T. "The New Jersey Sampler: Historic Tales of Old New Jersey." *New Jersey Almanac*. Upper Montclair, New Jersey, 1964.

———. *The New Jersey Shore*. New Brunswick, NJ: Rutgers University Press, 1958.

Dorsey, Leslie, and Janice Devine. *Fare Thee Well: A Backward Look at Two Centuries of Historic American Hostelries, Fashionable Spas and Seaside Resorts*. New York: Crown, 1964.

Dorwart, Jeffery M. *Cape May County, New Jersey: The Making of an American Resort Community*. New Brunswick, NJ: Rutgers University Press, 1992.

F. Sidney Townsend Diaries. Cape May County Historical Society Collection, Cape May, New Jersey.

Funnell, Charles E. *By the Beautiful Sea: The Rise and High Times of that Great American Resort, Atlantic City*. New Brunswick, NJ: Rutgers University Press, 1983.

History of Cape May, N.J., Section Base, U.S. Navy, World War One, Twenty-fifth Anniversary. Cape May, NJ, 1942.

Hollemon, Kenneth C. *From Whence We Came: A History of the Coast Guard in Southern New Jersey and Delaware*. N.p.: self-published, 1987.

MacDonald, H. Gerald. *The History of Railroad Transportation to Cape May, New Jersey*. Drexel Hill, PA: Keystone, Pennsylvania Railroad Technical and Historical Society, 1993.

Magrath, C.S. *Guide Book and Directory: Cape May and Cape May Point*. Cape May, NJ: self-published, 1881.

Mansion House letter, written from Cape Island, July 19, 1838. Cape May County Library Commission Collection, Cape May, New Jersey.

Mathewson, Craig C. "Cape May Steamboat Landing." *South Jersey Magazine* (Spring 1991).

Pitts, Carolyn, Michael Fish, Hugh J. McCauley and Trina Vaux. *The Cape May Handbook*. Philadelphia, PA: Athenaeum of Philadelphia, 1977.

Poulson's Advertiser. "Cape Town: Narrative of Cape May." August 1823.

Rinhart, Floyd, and Marion Rinhart. *Summertime: Photographs of Americans at Play, 1850–1900*. New York: Clarkson N. Potter, 1978.

Savadore, Larry, and Margaret Thomas Buchholz. *Great Storms of the Jersey Shore*. Harvey Cedars, NJ: Down the Shore Publishing and the SandPaper, 1993.

Bibliography

Stevens, Lewis Townsend. *The History of Cape May County, New Jersey from the Aboriginal Times to the Present Day*. Cape May, NJ: self-published, 1897.

Thomas, George E., and Carl Doebley. *Cape May: Queen of the Seaside Resorts*. Cranbury, NJ: Associated University Press, 1976.

Vanderbilt, Arthur T. *Fortune's Children: The Fall of the House of Vanderbilt*. New York: William Morrow, 1989.

Wentzel, Don. "100th Anniversary of Cape May's Second Railroad." *South Jersey Magazine* (Summer 1994).

———. "The Railroad Comes to Cape Island." *South Jersey Magazine* (Spring 1982).

West Jersey Railroad Company booklet. Cape May, New Jersey, 1877.

Wheeler, Edward S. *Scheyichbi and the Strand: Early Days Along the Delaware*. Philadelphia, PA: J.B. Lippincott, 1876.

Wilson, Harold F. *The Jersey Shore: A Social and Economic History*. New York: Lewis Historical Publishing Company, 1953.

Woolman, H.C., and T.T. Price. *Historical and Biographical Atlas of the New Jersey Coast*. Philadelphia, PA: self-published, 1878.

Newspapers

Atlantic City Press
Cape May County Gazette
Cape May County Herald
Cape May County Times
Cape May Star and Wave
Cape May Wave
Christian Beacon Press
Illustrated London News
Independent Record
New York Herald
Ocean Wave
Paulson's Advertiser
Pennsylvania Gazette
Philadelphia Daily Aurora
Philadelphia Daily Times

Bibliography

Philadelphia Evening Bulletin
Philadelphia Evening Telegraph
Philadelphia Inquirer
Philadelphia Sunday Dispatch
Richmond Dispatch
Richmond Whig
Star-Ledger
Star of the Cape

INDEX

A

Abbey guesthouse 168
Absecon Island 35
Admiral Hotel Company 122
Alabama capitol building 88
American Bracketed Villa style 94
America's Cup 67
amusement rides 86, 106
  Epicycloidal Swing 86
  Ferris wheel 86
"angel" parking program 171
Ash Wednesday Storm 152
Atlantic City, New Jersey 35, 36, 48, 56, 67, 69, 85, 86, 89, 92, 107, 112, 115, 123, 128, 131, 170
Atlantus (concrete ship) 130, 131

B

Baltimore, Maryland 17, 22, 35, 41, 67, 113
Barrett's tenpin alley 79
baseball 58
beach erosion 99, 100, 137

bed-and-breakfast phenomenon 66, 169, 170
Benjamin Franklin Bridge 132
Bethlehem Steel Company (testing ground) 125, 127
Big House. *See* hotels (Congress Hall)
Boston 11, 12, 130
Bowman, John, Jr. 18
Boyton, Peter Paul 60, 62
Bradshaw, Chief 77
Bramble, Edwin C. 164, 166
Brandy Station, Virginia 43, 45
Buchanan, James 37
Bullitt, John C. 50, 51, 54, 66, 88
Burns, Captain J.H. 17
Burnside, General Ambrose 44
Button, Stephen Decatur 50, 51, 54, 66, 87, 88, 93, 95, 96

C

Cahill, William T. 164
Cain, Philip 32, 33
Cake, J.F. 48, 67
Camden, New Jersey 13, 34, 35, 36, 53, 74, 75, 135

INDEX

Cape Henlopen, Delaware 41, 128
Cape Henlopen Light, Delaware 20
Cape Island Baptist 124
Cape Island Base Ball Club 59
Cape Island Creek 100, 151
Cape Island Home Guard (Civil War) 40
Cape Island Road 13
Cape Island Turnpike Company (Sunset Boulevard) 34
Cape May Athletic Club 108
Cape May Automobile Club 118
Cape May Beach Land Company 100
Cape May Board of Commissioners 56, 64
Cape May Board of Trade 112
Cape May boom 131
Cape May Canal 136, 137
Cape May City Land Company 100
Cape May City Progressive League 131
Cape May Cottagers Association 107, 164
Cape May Driving Park 105
Cape May Hotel Company 121
Cape May/Lewes Ferry 113, 132, 153
Cape May Light and Power 121
Cape May Lighthouse 20
Cape May Point 18, 97, 98, 100, 101, 102, 104, 128, 131
Cape May Real Estate Company 113, 114, 117, 119, 121, 125
Cape May Section Base No. 9 125
Catholic Diocese of Camden 162
Centennial Exposition 67
Chamberlain Hospitality Group 157

charter, Cape May 54, 64
Chevrolet, Louis 118
Civil War 39, 43, 56, 58, 66, 67, 87, 96, 98, 154
Clay, Henry 26, 27
Clemson College conference 158
coastal dim-out (World War II) 134, 136, 137
Coast Guard Section Base No. 9 127
Cold Spring jetties. *See* beach erosion
colonial roads 13
Cone, Jonathan 102
Congress Place 88, 162
conservative politics (Cape May City) 94, 106, 107, 136, 148, 149, 154, 155
Convention Hall 126, 140, 144, 151, 161, 175
"Cool Cape May" campaign 127
Cooledge, Harold Norman, Jr. 158, 159
Cooper's Ferry, New Jersey 13
cottages
  Atlantic Terrace 93
  Denizot's Sea View 75
  Edward Morris 51
  Edward Warne 51
  Fryer 75
  John Benezet 51
  King's 78
  Lafayette 154
  Ludlam 79
  Ocean View 93
  Oliver Smith 51
  Samuel Harrison 51
  Stockton Row 66, 79
  Weightman 75, 154
  Wolf 79
  Wyoming 80, 94

INDEX

Crowley, Dale (preacher) 154
Culver, N.H. (architect) 97
Cunningham, John T. (historian) 144

D

Delaware and Raritan Canal 36
Denizot, Victor 75, 88, 93, 95
Dennis's Creek 13
Department of Housing and Urban Development (HUD) 160
Devine, Elizabeth 98, 99, 100
Devine, Mark 98, 99
Driving Park Association 105
Du Bois, W.E.B. 28
Duffy, Charles 48

E

East Cape May Improvement Company 113
Edmunds, James 105
Edwards, Frank 114
Eldridge Johnson house. *See* Pink House
Elephantine Colossus 97
Emlen Physick Mansion 166, 169
Evans, Joseph 88
Excelsior Hot and Cold Baths 75
excursion house 53, 54, 56, 67, 85, 98, 101, 104, 116. *See also* hotels (Sea Breeze)

F

Fairthorne, Frederick 50, 51
ferry scheme. *See* Rosenfeld, Jesse
fires
  1869 60, 62, 65, 66, 69, 75, 85
  1878 73, 85, 87, 88, 93, 149
  American Hotel 62
  Mansion House 36
  Mount Vernon Hotel 32, 33, 36
  New Atlantic 62
  New Columbia 108
  United States Hotel 40, 62, 63
  Windsor 160
First Baptist Church, Cape May 124
Fite, Ray 161
Flinn, William 113
Flynn, Captain 45, 46
Ford, Henry 118, 126
Fort, George E. 119
Fort Mifflin 19
Fort Sumter 39
Foster, Frank T. 32
fun factory (Sewell's Point) 121, 125
Furness, Frank 71

G

Garden State Parkway 143
Gauvry, Frank A. 164
General Jackson 14
Glassboro, New Jersey 13
Grant Street Summer Station 67, 71, 102, 104
Graves, Nelson Zuinglius 121
Great Atlantic Hurricane 139
Great March Storm 152, 153, 158

H

Hallenhack, Mrs. 87
Hand, Aaron W. 112
Hand, Amelia 47
Heinan, Anton 128
Higbee's Beach 125
Hildreth, F.H. 108
Hildreth, George 94
Historic District Commission 163, 166
Historic Preservation Commission 171
Holly House guesthouse 168

INDEX

Hotel Cape May Cup 119
hotels
  Admiral 133, 153
  American 62
  American House 28
  Arctic 69
  Arlington 71
  Atlantic 23, 24, 49, 51, 60, 69, 74, 75, 80, 81, 84, 93
  Atlantic Hall 16, 17, 21, 22, 24, 25
  Avenue 81
  Baltimore Inn 110, 161
  Brexton 113
  Brunswick House 93
  Cape Island House 28
  Carroll Villa 94, 95
  Centre House 26, 49, 51, 69, 74, 75, 78, 81
  Chalfonte 46, 67, 69, 110, 113, 144
  Christian Admiral 153, 154, 155, 156, 157, 173
  Colonial 111, 113, 141, 144, 161
  Columbia 48, 50, 51, 58, 60, 62, 78, 79, 81, 88, 141
  Columbia House 28, 49, 51, 79
  Commercial House 28, 49
  Congress Hall 21, 22, 23, 24, 26, 34, 41, 42, 48, 49, 51, 52, 53, 58, 66, 67, 69, 71, 73, 74, 81, 84, 88, 93, 96, 110, 113, 116, 128, 141, 144, 153, 156, 157, 160, 173
  Considine 49
  Continental 48, 49, 74
  Cottage by the Sea 49
  Delaware Bay House 101
  Delaware House 28, 49, 108
  Ebbitt 157. *See also* hotels (Virginia)
  Franklin House 28
  Greenwood 49
  Hotel Cape May 117, 118, 119, 121, 122, 126, 133, 153, 173
  Hotel Dale 28
  Hughes Hall 28
  Knickerbocker 75
  Lafayette 88, 95, 96, 110, 113, 141, 144, 155, 161
  La Pierre House 49
  Madison House 28
  Mansion House 22, 23, 24, 26, 27
  Marine Villa 110, 113
  Merchants, the 49, 51, 69, 74, 81, 94
  Metropolitan House 49
  Mount Vernon 29, 30, 32, 33, 36, 52, 98, 99
  National 49, 69
  New Atlantic 25, 26, 63, 65
  New Columbia 94, 108
  New Jersey House 28
  New Stockton Villa 124, 143
  Ocean Breeze 49
  Ocean House 26, 49, 69, 73, 74, 75, 79, 81, 84
  Old Atlantic 26
  Proskauer's Maison Dorce 58
  Reigel's New Cottage 58
  Sea Breeze 53, 56, 69, 85, 98, 115, 116
  Sherman House 50, 69, 93
  Star Villa (Morning Star/Evening Star) 95, 155, 161
  St. Charles 69
  Stockton 54, 55, 56, 58, 66, 68, 73, 79, 85, 87, 95, 96, 113, 124
  Surf House 49, 51
  Tontine Hall 37, 49
  Tremont House 49

INDEX

United States 49, 51, 60, 62, 69, 93
Virginia 113, 153, 157
Washington House 49, 51
White Hall 28, 49
Windsor 88, 93, 96, 110, 113, 144, 153, 160
Hudson, Henry 144
Hughes, Ellis 14, 16, 21
Hughes's tavern 14, 16
Hughes, Thomas H. 21
Hunt, Richard Morris 88
Hunt's Pier 140

I

improvement ticket (railroad) 54, 58
iron pier (Cape May) 104, 113, 126

J

Jackson's Clubhouse 66
Jacob Jones 133
jersey/shore wagons 13
Johnson, Andrew 49
Johnson, Lyndon B. 160
Jones, Paul (columnist) 143

K

Kansas-Nebraska Act 34
Kersal 26, 27. *See also* hotels (Mansion House)
Kickapoo 127
King George III 12
Knight, E.C. 93
Kromer, John 71

L

Lafferty, James V. 97
Large House. *See* hotels (Congress Hall)
Lazaretto, the 19

Leach, Joseph S. 34, 39, 41, 42, 47, 56
Leach, Josiah Granville 42
Lee, General Robert E. 45
Lee, General William Henry Fitzhugh 45
Lehman's Mill, New Jersey 13
Lewistown, Delaware 41
Libby Prison 46. *See also* Sawyer, Henry W.
"Liberty Special" 126
lighthouse history 20
"Light of Asia" 97, 98
Lincoln, Abel 27, 28
Lincoln, Abraham 27, 38, 45
Little, Albert B. 98
Long Branch, New Jersey 50, 56, 69, 107, 170
"Lottery of Death" 44, 45, 46
Ludlam, Richard Smith 22, 26, 79
Ludlam, Samuel R. 79, 84

M

Magonagle, Samuel 56, 57
Mainstay guesthouse 168
Malago Mill, New Jersey 13
Marcus Hook 19
Margate elephant 97
Market Street Wharf, Philadelphia 14
Mason-Dixon line 35
McAllister, Miss Sarah A. 23
McCollum, Peter 51
McCreary, Senator John B. 66, 87
McIntire, Carl 122, 153, 154, 155, 156, 157, 161
McMakin, Benjamin 25
McMakin, John 65
McMakin, Joseph 24, 25
Mid-Atlantic Center for the Arts (MAC) 166, 167, 169

185

INDEX

Miller, Aaron 69
Miller, Waters B. 40
Mills, Ephraim 16
Mills, Mary 16
Millville, New Jersey 13
Minnix, Bruce 167
Mooney, James 94
Morning Star (sloop) 14
mosquito problem 108, 124
Mount Vernon Hotel and Lot Association 99
Mount Vernon Hotel Company 29, 35
Mount Vernon Land Company 98, 99, 106
Murtagh, Bill 160

N

National Navigation Company 130
National Trust for Historic Preservation 144, 160
naval hospital (World War I) 126
Needles, Henry 161
Nelson Z. Graves (dredge) 121
Neptune Land Company 98
New Castle, Delaware 17, 19, 35, 71
New Jersey Department of Environmental Protection 166
New Jersey Newport 121, 122
newspapers, Cape May history of 34, 56, 58, 92, 97
New York 11, 12, 22, 67

O

Ocean City, New Jersey 123
Ocean Villa 95
Ogden, L.C. 124
Olden, Governor Charles 40
Osterling, Frederick J. 121

P

Page, Joseph E. 50
Parsons, Robert 12
Pea Patch 19
Pennsylvania Globe Gas Light Company 92
Pennyland Pier 141
Philadelphia Centennial Committee 67
Philadelphia, Pennsylvania 11, 12, 13, 14, 17, 21, 22, 24, 26, 28, 29, 34, 35, 36, 37, 40, 47, 48, 49, 51, 53, 58, 67, 71, 86, 101, 113, 114, 117, 123, 131, 132, 135
Phoenix Iron Company 105
Physick, Emlen 71
Pierce, Franklin 34
Pink House 162
Pitney, Dr. Jonathan 35, 36
Pittsburgh (dredge) 116, 119
Pittsburgh Syndicate 114
Pitts, Carolyn 163, 164, 166
Port Elizabeth 13
Port Penn 17

Q

Queen Anne Connection 113, 128
Queen Anne style 94

R

Radio Free America 155
railroads
  Atlantic City 109
  Camden and Amboy 36
  Camden and Atlantic 35, 104
  Cape May 109
  Cape May and Millville 47, 51
  Cape May and Sewell's Point 104
  Cape May, Delaware Bay and Sewell's Point 104, 125

INDEX

Conrail 133
Delaware Bay and Cape May 102, 104
Delaware Bay and Sewell's Point 104
Millville and Glassboro Railroad Company 47
Pennsylvania 104, 109, 116, 133, 135
Pennsylvania-Reading Seashore Lines 135
Philadelphia and Reading 116, 117
Queen Anne 113
Reading 109, 133, 135
South Jersey 109, 110
Tuckahoe and Cape May 109
West Jersey 51, 54, 64, 67, 88, 102, 104, 109
West Jersey and Atlantic 110
West Jersey and Seashore 104, 110, 126
Ralston, Mrs. 71
Reading Company 135
Red Cross Disaster Force 141
Reeves, C.B. 93
Reger, Theodore M. 97, 98, 106
Richmond, Virginia 35
Rosenfeld, Jesse 128, 131, 132
"rum row" 127

S

Sandford, J.B. 116
Sandman, Charles 164
Savage, Lieutenant Commandant USNR Frederick A. 125
Savannah, Georgia 35
Sawyer, Captain Henry W. 43, 44, 45, 46, 67
Schellinger's Landing 12, 34, 116, 126

Scott, Senator I. Grant 135
sea-bathing 12, 14, 21, 22, 27, 29, 30, 60, 89
Sea Isle City, New Jersey 108
Sewell's Point 104, 118, 121, 125
Sewell, William 54
Sewell, William, Jr. 121
Shelton College 154, 155
Shields, Peter 121
"shoobies" 52, 53
"six-bitters" (Coast Guard cutters) 127
South Cape May 99, 100, 106, 131, 141, 151
Starr, Dr. Walter 119
Steamboat Landing Turnpike 100
steamboats
   America 28
   Delaware 17, 19
   Mountaineer 28
   Napoleon 28
   New Brunswick 113
   Republic 71, 101, 131
   Traveler 28
   Vesta 17
steamboat travel 17, 18, 19, 21, 26, 28, 34, 35, 36, 37, 42, 53, 71, 101, 102, 131
Stockton Bath Houses 79, 161
Stockton, Commodore Robert 55
Stockton, Senator 55
Storm of the Century 152
Sunset Beach, Cape May Point 131
Sunset Boulevard 18, 34, 98, 100, 131

T

taverns, colonial 14, 16, 21
Tenenbaum, Dr. Irving 146, 148, 160, 166
Tenenbaum, Howard 144

INDEX

Thurmond, Senator Strom 154
Townsend, F. Sidney 98, 101, 105, 108
Twentieth Century Reformation House broadcast 154. *See also* McIntire, Carl

U

U-boat attacks 133, 135, 137
Urban Renewal Administration 160
U.S. Naval Annex 121, 133

V

Vanderbilt family 87, 88
Victorian Lace guesthouse 168
Victorian Towers 162
Victorian Village 160, 161, 166
Vigilance Committee 40

W

Ward, Michael 94
Warne's Drugstore 79
Washington, Booker T. 28
Washington, D.C. 22, 35, 41, 48, 160
Washington Street pedestrian mall 161
Weatherby tract 98, 100
Weightman, William, Sr. 154
Welsbach Gaslight Company of Baltimore, Maryland 146
West, John 29
Whildin, Captain 19
White House Tea Room 140
Whitney, Thomas 93
Wildwood, New Jersey 123, 159, 174
Willard Hotel, Washington, D.C. 48
Williamson, Thomas H. 98

Wilmington, Delaware 19, 71
Wilson, Woodrow 125
Winder, General John H. 45
Winslow Junction 108
Wissahickon Naval Training Barracks 126, 127
Woodbury, New Jersey 13
Woodruff's Silver Palace drawing room coaches 52
Woolman, Samuel 32
Wright, Walter C., Jr. 148, 162

Y

Youngberg, Carl R. 144

Z

ZR-2 (dirigible) 128

About the Author

Emil R. Salvini served two terms as a member of the Cape May City Preservation Commission and is a life member of the Cape May County Historical Society. He is the author of *Hobey Baker, American Legend*—honored by the New Jersey Council for the Humanities—and the acclaimed *Boardwalk Memories: Tales of the Jersey Shore* and *Jersey Shore: Vintage Images of Bygone Days*. This versatile historian is both a careful scholar and an excellent storyteller. He created and hosts the popular PBS series *Tales of the Jersey Shore*. A graduate of William Paterson University and Harvard University, he lives with his wife in Wayne, New Jersey, and together they stroll the boardwalks as often as possible.

Visit us at
www.historypress.net